simply®

tea leaf
reading

JACQUELINE TOWERS

STERLING/ZAMBEZI
An imprint of Sterling Publishing Co., Inc.

New York / London
www.sterlingpublishing.com

dedication

In loving memory
of my great-grandmother Dorothy Young

STERLING and the distinctive Sterling logo are registered trademarks of
Sterling Publishing Co., Inc.

Library of Congress Cataloging-in-Publication Data Available

2 4 6 8 10 9 7 5 3 1

Published by Sterling Publishing Co., Inc.
387 Park Avenue South, New York, NY 10016
Copyright © 2008 by Jacqueline Towers
Published in the UK solely by Zambezi Publishing Ltd
P.O. Box 221, Plymouth, Devon, PL2 2YJ UK
Distributed in Canada by Sterling Publishing
c/o Canadian Manda Group, 165 Dufferin Street
Toronto, Ontario, Canada M6K 3H6
Distributed in Australia by Capricorn Link (Australia) Pty. Ltd.
P.O. Box 704, Windsor, NSW 2756, Australia

Illustrations from the Rider-Waite Tarot Deck® reproduced by permission
of U.S. Games Systems, Inc., Stamford, CT 06902 USA.
Copyright ©1971 by U.S. Games Systems, Inc. Further reproduction prohibited.
The Rider-Waite Tarot Deck® is a registered trademark of U.S. Games Systems, Inc.

Illustrations on pages 16–19 and 121 by Tina Fong
Illustrations of black leaf reading in Chapter 8 by Adam Raiti
Illustrations on chapter openers, of astrological signs,
and of the alphabet, except for the letter O, by Hannah Firmin

Sterling ISBN-13: 978-1-4027-4487-7
ISBN-10: 1-4027-4487-0
Zambezi ISBN-13: 978-1-903065-56-3
ISBN-10: 1-903065-56-9

For information about custom editions, special sales, premium and
corporate purchases, please contact Sterling Special Sales Department
at 800-805-5489 or specialsales@sterlingpublishing.com.

contents

THE CATEGORIES OF TEA
CAMELLIA SINENSIS

GREEN	OOLONG	BLACK (Red)
Non-fermented	Semi-fermented	Fully Fermented

Lightly Fermented   Heavily Fermented

WHITE	YELLOW	COMPRESSED (BLACK)
Steamed	Stacked	Tea Bricks Bowl Tea

introduction

Many people will remember hearing about a great-grandmother or a great-aunt who read tea leaves, and some of you might even be old enough to remember seeing tea leaf reading during your own life-time. Indeed, some of you might have had such a reading.

While tea leaf reading has become an unusual activity, coffee ground reading is still popular. Not surprisingly, tea leaf reading was once popular in Northern Europe, while coffee ground reading is a Spanish, Portuguese, Turkish, Greek, and Middle Eastern skill. People still read coffee grounds in those countries and in the countries where the descendants of these people live. Thus we can find coffee ground readers in the Middle East, in the United States, and in Central and South America. Tea leaf reading probably originated in China, but it did so far back in time that one can't be categorical about its origins. Coffee ground reading seems to have orig-inated in Turkey.

So why should people read leaves and grounds rather than other things? Why not read coins, peanuts, clouds in the sky, or anything else? The truth is that intuitive people can "read" just about anything. For example, it used to be common for people to "read" the flames in the fire as the coal or wood burned in the household hearth. Africans still read messages from the shapes in clouds, as well as read-ing stones, shells, bones, and seeds. In Europe, there were specialist readers who asked their "clients" to bring them a few dried leaves, and then crumple them in their hands and let them fall onto the ground, so that the "reader" could then read the shapes. My friend David Bingham sometimes amuses his friends with this party trick: he asks a questioner to crumple up a packet of potato chips, then open it and pour the contents out onto a plate. David then reads the crumbs.

So, we discover that a good psychic can "read" anything. When it comes to reading shapes, the best readers are those with an artistic eye, who can see shapes forming that look like boats, trees, rabbits, and the like. Once the reader has a mental dictionary of a few dozen shapes in his head, he can give a reading. For instance, if drifting pieces of cloud, pieces of dried leaf, a darting flame in the fireplace, or a few potato chip crumbs can look like some-thing, how much easier it is to read the shapes made by tea leaves!

One major difference between tea leaf and coffee ground reading and these other ancient forms of divination is that the "questioner" must hold the cup in her hands, and she must drink from it. This means that the questioner must hold the cup and its contents within the innermost part of her aura for around ten or fifteen minutes. Indeed, if you think about it, a little bit of the cup will have entered the boundaries of the questioner's body. This means that the questioner will transfer her vibes to the cup and its contents in a very personal way. This creates a more personal contact than merely shuffling a deck of cards, and goodness knows there are enough people giving highly successful card readings around the world these days.

So can anyone learn to read the leaves? Yes, anyone can. Obviously those who have an artistic eye will pick this skill up more quickly than someone who is not so artistic. Having said that, it is a matter of practice before even the least artistic person can pick up the skill. One tip here is not try too hard, but to allow your eyes to go slightly out of focus for a while as you gaze into the cup. After this, sharpen your focus again, and you will find the leaves almost gathering together in the cup (or in your mind) to create shapes and symbols.

DO YOU NEED TO BE PSYCHIC?

When reading the tea leaves, will you need to call upon your psychic ability? Not really, but the more you read for others, the more your intuition and psychism will develop. And the more it develops, the better you will become at reading the leaves. You will probably have no psychic or intuitive feelings at first, but that's where the tea leaf dictionary in this book comes into its own. All you need to do is to pick out the shapes and look them up in the dictionary, and you will then be able to give anyone a reading. But if you keep going and if you read for more and more people, you find yourself in a kind of reverse Catch-22 situation. The Catch-22 theory is like a nightmare, where whatever you try to do is stymied; but the reverse of this is that the more you do, the more you can do. Your ability will grow in various ways. First, you will find the shapes gathering together more quickly in your mind's eye; and second, you will start to build up a repertoire of leaf meanings in your own mind. The more obvious ones, such as those connected with relationships (rings) and those concerned with money (dots) or travel (train lines and vehicles) will be the first to stick. As you go on, your psychic ability will grow—and as long as you allow it to come through, it will do so.

WHAT IS PSYCHIC ABILITY?

Psychic ability is the advanced use of intuition. Being psychic is as natural as breathing. We are all psychic to some extent; all it takes is a willingness to become aware of this, and to act on what one begins to notice. So let's look at the psychic side of things, in the specific context of tea leaf reading. The most common reasons for people to develop their psychic gifts are for channeling messages from "the other side," for healing, or for reading tarot cards, or perhaps as an aid in some other form of divination. However, the main thing that you will need to develop is your ability to visualize shapes, and that ability will soon start to translate itself into true clairvoyance.

ARE YOU ALREADY PSYCHIC?

There are four groups of psychic ability and you may fit into one or more of them, because it would be a very rare person who would not be able to fit into of one these groups. The four types of psychic sense are psychic feeling, psychic intuition, psychic hearing, and psychic vision. The best-known psychic sense is clairvoyance, or psychic vision. Clairvoyants are psychics who see images or pictures. Clairvoyant literally means '"clear-seeing," so the clairvoyant psychic must learn to interpret the pictures or images that he sees.

HOW DO YOU DEVELOP YOUR ABILITIES?

An open-minded attitude is essential to our being able to receive (and distinguish) anything. There has to be a willingness to respond to nonphysical stimulus, and an ability to trust the information received. So why not become an optimist, allow yourself to be psychic, and trust yourself sufficiently to use the natural ability that is in you?

Most of those who say they are amateur or professional psychics have recognized the signs at some previous point in their lives, and they have focused their attention on their workings. Such people became familiar with the presence of the subtle kind of energy that is involved, and perhaps in what we might call a "sixth sense." There must be both a desire and willingness to develop and tune in to what people see or receive. If you want to develop your psychic talents, you will need to practice them. Fortunately, this is an extremely interesting thing to do, and it can be great fun at times.

You need to be relaxed to perform at the optimal level; therefore, you must learn to meditate, because you will develop far more quickly if you practice meditation. Meditation is extremely important. Not only does it help you to clear your mind and to focus on what you are trying to achieve, but it also helps your body to relax. If you have never meditated before, you should sit in a comfortable chair and relax. Just let your thoughts drift, and think of nothing in particular. The important thing is that you take the time to clear your mind.

FOR HOW LONG SHOULD YOU MEDITATE?

If you have never practiced meditation before and wish to practice regularly, it is best to start meditating for ten to fifteen minutes once a day. After a while, you may want to increase this to twenty minutes once a day or ten minutes twice a day. Meditation taps into some very powerful inner energies, and this will become apparent with practice.

CHOOSING A DIVINATION

Divination is a broad term that includes fortune telling, precognition, prophesy, tarot reading, and other methods used in an effort to predict the future. To learn a divination is the first step in developing psychic ability. Tasseography, or reading the tea leaves, is the perfect way to do this.

Psychics talk about "tuning in" to their clients, but visual objects help clairvoyants to focus their thoughts and to have something to focus on, while creating the link. This is where tasseography comes into its own. Tasseography is a divination that enables you to examine tea leaves and to interpret shapes and patterns. When you begin to look into the cup, the shapes and patterns you see may seem to be random, but if you relax and allow yourself to slip into a meditative state, the shapes will start to become clear. The guidelines and the interpretations contained within this book will help you to understand the meanings behind the shapes and to develop the importance of what you are seeing.

While you are learning, try to find someone who is patient and understanding to act as a "guinea pig." Take your time, because there is no use in trying to force the information to come through. It time, you may find that you go beyond just reading and interpreting the shapes in the cup, as your intuitive and psychic powers start to grow. Even if you become a true clairvoyant, you will still find it useful to start your reading by giving your "client" a cup of tea and then looking at the shapes, because even the best clairvoyants often need a nudge before their "client's" stories start to flow.

The role of a psychic often goes beyond just giving messages or making predications. Psychics need compassion and good communication skills if they are to act upon the information that they see or receive. Please remember, you are dealing with people's emotions. There are many people worldwide who perform predications and have psychic abilities, and you are just someone who is awakening those skills. This thought will serve you well, so be modest and have respect for those you are able to read for and you will develop.

So, let us now return to the main purpose of this book and ask the following questions:

- Can reading tea leaves and coffee grounds help a person to become psychic?
- What use is this skill to someone who is already psychic?

Offering tea and coffee cup readings to others will definitely help you to develop and expand your psychic abilities. For example, the late Gordon Arthur Smith was one of the founding members of the prestigious British Astrological and Psychic Society, and his talent started to develop when his grandmother taught him to read tea leaves. Those who are already psychic often find it a strain to give readings by means of pure clairvoyance or clairaudience, so they like to use an aid that helps them to relax, tune in, and get the message across to their client. It is helpful to share a drink before the sitting and then take the cup from the "client" and let the contents work on the psychic's imagination, so that it kick-starts the process.

Oh, and enjoy your tea leaf readings.

ABOUT TEA LEAF
AND COFFEE READING

Tea is made of a particular kind of camellia plant, the *Camellia sinensis*. The people of China, the birthplace of tea, were keen to keep the secret of the tea plant within their borders, but a Portuguese adventurer smuggled a few small plants out, thus starting the growth and use of tea in many parts of the world. Most tea is grown in China and various parts of the Indian subcontinent, including Sri Lanka, but some grows in such unexpected places as Queensland in Australia and Cornwall in England. Naturally, we all know the story of the Boston Tea Party, which turned the United States from a potentially tea-drinking country to a coffee lover's paradise. Coffee originated from beans that were discovered in Ethiopia. Coffee cultivation and its use spread to Persia, Turkey, and the Arab world and eventually to Europe and the Americas.

Tasseomancy is a very old form of divination that is becoming popular once again. More commonly known as tea leaf reading, tasseomancy is a form of fortune-telling that uses the shapes left in a cup by tea leaves or coffee grounds. Tea leaf reading is much older than and requires more imagination than the tarot because there are no set-piece illustrations for the reader to draw on. The origins of the method came into being during the Middle Ages, when readers or diviners used a form of divination by wax, which was called "ceroscopy." Fine wax was melted in a brass vessel and then slowly poured into a bowl of cold water so that the wax immediately formed shapes, which the reader interpreted for the client. A similar form of divination was "molybdomancy," in which molten lead or tin was dripped into cold water.

Note: The word "tasseomancy," meaning "tea leaf reading," comes from the Arabic *tas*, meaning "cup" (which is taken from the French *tasse*, also meaning "cup") and the Greek suffix *-mancy*, meaning "prophecy."

Like tea itself, tasseomancy originated in ancient China, but it became associated with Gypsies, who later started the spread of the practice around the world. While witches were persecuted in the seventeenth and early eighteenth centuries, tasseomancy was still widely practiced because it didn't require the use of unusual tools or objects that would have marked the practitioner as a witch. Everyone had tea and a teapot in the home, so nobody could be accused of witchcraft just for owning those items. In England after 1735, witchcraft was no longer a capital offense, so people gradually started to take an interest in various forms of divination once again. The nineteenth and early twentieth centuries were particularly fertile times for all forms of fortune-telling, and this surge was jump-started in France as a result of Napoléon's interest in all things occult. In the later twentieth century, tea leaf reading fell out of fashion, probably due to the rise in popularity of fortune-telling cards. Tea leaf reading and coffee ground reading are now regaining popularity all around the world.

This book describes tea leaf interpretation, but there are many parts of the world where people prefer to read coffee grounds. The technique shown in this book can be applied to tea, coffee, herbal tea, soup in a cup, or anything else that leaves a residue after the liquid has been drunk. So let us now discover how to read tea leaves and similar residues for ourselves.

2

HOW TO MAKE TEA

THE TEAPOT

To read someone's tea leaves, you must first prepare a pot of tea the old-fashioned way, which means using loose tea and a teapot. You need a teapot that does not have an internal strainer, and you mustn't use a strainer when pouring the tea. The teapot can be plain or fancy, and it doesn't need to be made of any special material; an inexpensive glass, metal, or pottery teapot is fine.

THE TEA

You also need a packet of loose tea. You can use any kind of tea, but the reading might be easier if you use tea that has rather large leaf pieces. Examples include Darjeeling tea,

Assam tea, or any kind of Chinese tea. You can prepare the tea to suit your own taste; for instance, English style, with milk and sugar or sweetener; Russian style, with lemon and sugar; Chinese style, with jasmine flowers; or just tea on its own, strong or weak. Fruit tea or any other tea that has leaves and bits of the tea plant in it is fine.

Begin by warming the pot, which will make the tea brew nicely. Pour a little boiling water into the teapot, and then pour the hot water back out of the pot into the sink. Next put one teaspoon of tea per cup into the warmed teapot. Fill the teapot with freshly boiled water and stir the tea for a few seconds with a tall spoon to "elevate" the tea. Allow the tea to steep for two to five minutes. The tea will become stronger the longer it steeps, so if you or your questioner don't like "stewed" tea, don't let it sit in the pot too long. Stir the tea once again just before pouring. If you want to keep the teapot and its contents warm so that you can enjoy another cup a bit later, you might wish to invest in a tea cozy. If the tea becomes too strong or tastes stewed, you can add a little more boiling water to refresh it.

THE CUP AND SAUCER

A mug is not good for tea leaf reading; you need an old-fashioned cup and saucer. The cup should not be fluted or fancy and should be free of interior decoration. Indeed, the plainer the better, and a white cup with a white interior that is not too narrow is the best.

The cup and saucer can be made of inexpensive pottery or fine china, but it's better not to use a valuable antique, so it doesn't get damaged.

PREPARING FOR THE READING

Make the tea to suit the questioner's particular taste and then give it to her or him to drink. If the questioner takes sugar or needs to stir the drink for any other reason, provide a spoon and let her or him stir at will. Now let the questioner drink the tea, but while he or she does so, avoid chatting about anything personal or anything that might come up in the reading.

Once your questioner has finished drinking, take the cup and saucer, and then hold the cup in both your hands. Swill the dregs around three times in a counterclockwise direction, turn the cup so that the handle faces toward you, and get ready to read. Some practitioners suggest that you upend the cup into the saucer and then turn it around while it is on the saucer, giving it three twists in a counterclockwise direction before turning the cup upright again. You might wish to experiment with this method for both tea and coffee, as it might wash out too much of the material. Whatever method you choose, once you have the cup in your hands, turn it so that the handle is pointing toward you and prepare to read.

IT CAN ALL GO WRONG!

A colleague of mine, David Bingham, told me of his experience when he was working as a psychic giving readings in a shop. A lady came along and asked specifically for a tea leaf reading. Unfortunately, the shop's owner did not have the right kind of teacup; nor did he have a teapot or any loose tea. The shopkeeper went out and bought an expensive teapot, the correctly colored and shaped teacup and saucer, and some costly loose tea. He made the tea and the lady drank it, but when David came to read the tea leaves he discovered that there were none in the cup for him to read!

He ended up using all his psychic skills for the reading, along with a fair measure of guile to ensure that the lady could not see the leafless cup. After the reading, David asked the shopkeeper why there were no leaves in the cup. The man was totally perplexed until he and David inspected the pot. You can imagine the shopkeeper's annoyance to find, after having gone out specially and spending a small fortune on equipment, that the teapot had its own built-in strainer that had made the whole exercise rather pointless!

MAKING COFFEE

Many coffee readers like to use the Greek or Turkish type of coffee, as this allows a silt of fine grounds to remain in the cup. You will need to ask your questioner to leave some coffee in the cup after he or she has finished drinking, and then to turn the cup upside down onto the saucer and give it three short turns to the left. Then the questioner should upend the cup again and give it to you for interpretation. Alternatively, you may choose to make coffee from coarser grounds in a *cafetière* and pour a cupful out without using the strainer. Whichever method you choose, practice and a touch of intuition and imagination will make the reading work. The technique is the same as for a reading with tea leaves. The way the residue looks in the cup will depend upon the type of coffee that has been used and the method used to make the coffee. If you use Greek or Turkish fine-ground coffee, you will have to adapt your ideas and method to suit the material that you find in the cup.

3

PREPARATION AND TECHNIQUE

Most forms of fortune—telling combine a specific system, such as card or rune reading, with a measure of freewheeling intuitive or psychic impressionism, but you don't need to be born with any special gift to read tea leaves or coffee grounds. The questioner will leave his or her own traces and aura on the cup simply by holding it and drinking from it, and sooner or later, you will find yourself developing some measure of intuition and extra sensory perception. In the meanwhile, you will find that using this book to interpret the symbols that you see in the cup will be remarkably successful. Tea leaf or coffee ground reading is a little like dream interpretation because it takes a little imagination and a slightly artistic eye to do it successfully, but those who try it usually get the hang of it quite quickly.

LOCATION

The side of the cup and area closest to the handle represent the most personal area of the cup. This area can represent the inquirer, his or her home and family, and things that are close to the inquirer's heart or that relate personally to him or her. So in this part of the cup we can see events concerning the inquirer's health, personal feelings, loved ones, and immediate surroundings.

The side of the cup opposite the handle refers to strangers and to events that occur away from the home and family. Naturally, someone whose life is played out within the home will be more interested in the events marked on the handle side of the cup. Someone with no real interest in home and family will want to know more about the symbols that appear on the opposite side of the cup. Most people these days are interested in all aspects of life because we lead such busy and varied lives and many of us travel away from home from time to time.

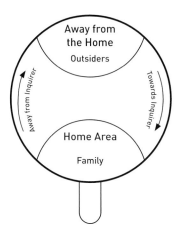

TIMING

There are two schools of thought with regard to determining the timing of the events you read in the teacup. The first idea is that the near future is shown by symbols that are close to the cup's rim, while the distant future is shown by symbols in the base of the cup. Anything close to both the rim and the handle depicts something that will happen almost immediately.

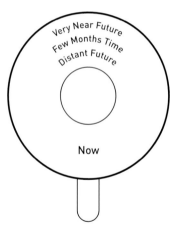

The second method splits the cup into two halves, with the left side representing the past and the right side representing the future. The recent past is shown by symbols that are close to the handle on the left-hand side, while the more distant past is represented by leaves that are farther from the handle on that side. The near future is shown by symbols that are close to the handle on the right side of the cup, while the more distant future is indicated by symbols that are farther from the handle on that side.

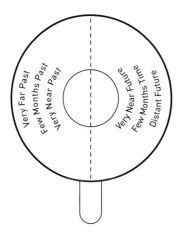

Whatever method you choose, you will read each symbol several times. You will need to look up the shape in the listing in this book to discover the meaning, and then consider its location and timing. Another factor to consider is the "happiness quotient," because symbols that are close to the cup's rim represent joyful events, while those close to the base of the cup represent sad ones. Even a truly nasty symbol, such as a gun or dagger, will be less harmful if it is closer to the cup's rim rather than farther down. Any remaining liquid in the cup symbolizes tears of sadness.

SOME HANDY HINTS

Here are some ideas that have come my way from various experienced tea leaf and coffee grounds readers.

- Check all the easily discernable symbols first. Look for initials, numbers, dots, and lines.
- Symbols pointing to the handle denote something that is approaching the inquirer, for example, a letter, a visitor, and so on.
- Symbols pointing away from the handle suggest that something or someone is going away from the questioner or from his or her home and family environs.
- Symbols that appear cloudy symbolize events whose meaning will become clear only with the passage of time.
- Large symbols suggest big events, while smaller ones denote less important ones.
- Symbols should never be interpreted in isolation, because the overall picture combines symbols in relation to one another, and due consideration should be given to the size, clarity, and position of each symbol.
- It is important to take into consideration the type of person for whom you are giving the reading. An older person with fixed ideas will have a different outlook on life compared to a younger person who has yet to form concrete views and opinions.

You might find it difficult to see anything in your teacup at first, but do not worry. The images are not clear like a photograph, and you may struggle to see much at first. Relax! Just allow your mind and imagination to come into play. Examine the cup once or twice, turn the cup, and then tip it toward you or away from you, looking at the tea leaves as you do so. Very soon you will be able to make out one image, then another, and before you know it the symbols will start to leap out at you.

SHOULD YOU READ FOR YOURSELF?

There is nothing to stop you from reading your own tea leaves, other than the fact that it is not an easy thing to do. You know too much about your own situation and are therefore inclined to put your own spin on the reading. Much the same goes for reading for a friend or loved one. However, we are all interested in our friends, our loved ones, and ourselves, and no harm can come from giving it a try.

THE BLOTTING-PAPER METHOD

The blotting-paper method is another way of reading tea leaves that you may not have known about.

To use this method, draw a representation of the inside of a teacup on a sheet of white blotting paper or a piece of kitchen paper towel. In other words, draw a large circle with a handle, and a smaller circle inside the larger one.

In the middle of the inner circle make a small hole.

Make a cup of tea and follow the instructions as before. Once the inquirer has finished drinking the tea, upend the remaining liquid in the cup over the diagram, ensuring that the handle of the cup aligns with the one on the diagram.

The majority of the liquid will run down the hole, leaving the tea leaves sitting on the surface. You can then interpret the symbols and shapes exactly as if they were in a cup. Any of the leaves that fall outside the circle, as well as the mass of tea leaves that collects around the hole, should be disregarded.

4

COMMON SYMBOLS AND IMAGES

Certain symbols turn up on a regular basis in a tea leaf reading, and while some of these are specific to tea leaf reading, others stem from other divinations. There are also some well-known superstitions surrounding tea and coffee.

SUPERSTITIONS

- When two spoons are accidentally placed in a saucer, there will be news of a birth.
- Too much liquid remaining in the cup traditionally represents tears and sadness.
- A single leaf floating on a full cup of tea means the inquirer will come into money.
- A single leaf stuck at the side of a full cup means that a stranger will come into the questioner's life. Check whether the stranger is the new boy or girl from next door or will come from near the home environs (close to the handle) or from a distance (the other side of the cup).
- Stalks always represent people. A long, firm stalk symbolizes a man, while a shorter, thinner stalk symbolizes a woman. If the stalk is straight, the stranger will be honest, but if it is bent, the stranger will be untrustworthy. The color of the stalk traditionally shows the color of the person's complexion and hair; for example, a light-colored stalk represents a fair person, a dark stalk represents a dark-haired person, and so on. If the stalk is slanted diagonally in the cup, the stranger's motives might not be honest or straightforward.

- Leaves piled up on the side of the cup always mean trouble. If the pile is close to the handle, the trouble will be of the questioner's own making; if the pile is on the side and close to the handle, the trouble will come from a familiar source, such as family, friends, work associates, and so on. If the pile is on the side of the cup that is opposite the handle, the trouble will come from an outside source.
- If someone pours tea and then another person goes on to pour from the same pot, there will be news of a birth within the next year.

I once had a friend whose mother-in-law used to say that if two people poured tea from the same pot, red-haired twins would be born within the next year. My friend's father-in-law was a redhead, and there were several sets of twins in her own family, so she was very careful about who poured what from her teapot. She said she had no objection to redheads, but she couldn't have coped with twins in addition to the two lively children that she already had!

GEOMETRIC SHAPES

Oddly enough, certain shapes have similar meanings in all psychic systems, even such "scientific" ones as astrology and palmistry.

- Circles represent the energy or power to influence events.
- They also symbolize the completion of projects and success, or things coming full circle.

- Circles can also represent wedding rings, but so few people marry nowadays that we usually refer to them as lovers' rings.
- A circle near the handle but at the bottom of the cup indicates a broken relationship. A circle that thins or breaks anywhere around its circumference is a definite indication of a break.
- Two circles foretell two important relationships.

- An arc or arch represents the start of an enduring relationship. Traditionally speaking, this means a happy marriage.
- Crosses indicate choices or dramatic changes. These changes might be for the better in the long run, but the changes may be difficult to cope with in the early stages.
- A cross that is halfway up the cup and well away from the handle represents a major change.
- Triangles usually foretell fortunate events as long as the apex is not pointing down. Triangles can symbolize success resulting from using one's talent wisely.
- A triangle that is sitting nicely on its base with the point facing up means that money is coming to the inquirer. This symbol can also represent a legacy, a meeting in connection with money, or a business matter that works to the inquirer's advantage. If the triangle's base faces up and its apex faces down, the questioner's luck is about to run out.
- Squares can represent protection but can also indicate restriction, so you have to interpret these symbols carefully. For instance, if there is a negative image in the cup but there is a square around it or near it, the questioner will be protected from the worst of its effects. Similarly, if the questioner is looking for love, a new job, a fresh start, the chance for travel, or anything else that involves

breaking old patterns, a lone square or one that is surrounding or near another image suggests that it will be a while before the desired change will come.

SYMBOLS FROM OTHER SYSTEMS OF DIVINATION

Hearts

Hearts symbolize the emotions and matters of the heart. It is worth checking out other images near the heart symbol to see whether they are positive or negative. This will tell you whether things are likely to go well or badly for the questioner's love life.

Clubs

Club shapes often refer to money but also frequently represent business matters, work, career, and getting on in life. Where these things are concerned, a club image is a particularly good omen. This is a good symbol to find in a cup, even if it related to something other than work or business.

Diamonds

Diamond shapes relate to letters, e-mails, phone calls, and news of an important nature. They also represent money and luck, especially in new ventures or new sources of income. Diamond shapes can imply that something strange but good is about to occur.

Spades

Spades signify the start of a period of bad luck. None of us want this for ourselves, nor do we want to see this in some-one else's life, but the nature of karma means that some bad things do happen. Anyway, without a little rain falling, how can we appreciate the sunshine when it comes?

Runic Symbols

You really need to keep a rune book on your bookshelf if you want to interpret runic symbols, as each rune has its own specific meaning. Just for example, a commonly found sym-bol in tea leaf reading is a straight vertical line. This is the rune that means "ice," and if this symbol appears, things will be "frozen," or on hold, for a while.

- Dots formed by little specs of tea or coffee usually mean that money is coming to the questioner, but they can also represent a journey if other parts of the reading support this interpretation.

- Larger dots represent money that is obtained by making an effort. Their position indicates when this money might arrive, and their size and number relate to the amount.
- Straight or smoothly curved lines represent creativity and projects that follow a definite course.
- Wavy or curved lines warn of uncertainty and a need for caution, careful thought, intelligent planning, and better direction and control.
- Mountains mean that the inquirer will soon have to make a great effort, but it will be worth it in the end.
- Clusters or groups of symbols symbolize the emotions. Their size and position show the extent of emotional responses to events, and associated patterns indicate whether happiness or sadness is involved.
- Poorly outlined symbols suggest indecision or obstacles that hinder progress or contentment.
- Numbers can represent time, such as minutes, hours, days, or weeks, depending upon the relative nature of the other symbols. You will find more about numbers as they relate to tea leaf reading in Chapter 7, "Letters and Numerals," in this book.
- Letters of the alphabet may refer to the initials of relatives, friends, or associates. The closer to the handle they appear, the more important they are. Refer to Chapter 7, "Letters and Numerals," for more about letters as they relate to tea leaf reading.
- One or two bells can symbolize a wedding.
- The image of a ball near the top of the cup and not far from the handle suggests that the inquirer will soon be experiencing a period of restlessness.

- The image of an eye that is close to the handle means that an important offer will shortly be made, and that it will require careful scrutiny. The questioner will need to proceed cautiously.
- A series of dots from the top to the bottom of the cup signify money. If they are close to the bottom of the cup, this means that money will come in slowly and over a period of time.
- A heart near the top of the cup but far away from the handle signifies love and financial gain.
- The image of the sun at the bottom of the cup indicates improvement in all areas and success in all endeavors, even though symbols at the bottom of the cup don't normally bring good news.
- An arrow near the top of the cup and quite close to the handle means that important news will arrive soon, but weapons can bring unpleasant news or can relate to an enemy, especially when the arrow points to the handle.
- A ladder that is far from the handle suggests that the questioner will have to make a sustained effort but that it will produce good results.
- A basket right by the handle means that there will soon be a welcome guest bearing gifts.

AND FINALLY . . .

Try to use your instincts to come up with shapes and meanings of your own. When reading the tea leaves, you will enter another dimension, so utilize your feelings to make a prediction, even when there seems to be no logical message in the cup.

Remember to look at all the easily discernible symbols first, such as initials, numbers, dots, leaf stalks, and lines; symbols that are indistinct are less important.

5

ASTROLOGICAL SYMBOLS

A lone astrological symbol could have several meanings; for example, it might refer to someone who was born under the sign in question coming into your life. It might represent an event or circumstance that is depicted by that sign, such as a change of address for the sign of Cancer. The symbol might signify a health matter, such as a problem with the knees in the case of a Capricorn symbol. Lastly, a zodiac sign could suggest a significant time of year, so you should also check out the dates given below.

DATES FOR THE SIGNS OF THE ZODIAC

Aries	March 21 to April 19
Taurus	April 20 to May 20
Gemini	May 21 to June 21
Cancer	June 22 to July 22
Leo	July 23 to August 22
Virgo	August 23 to September 22
Libra	September 23 to October 22
Scorpio	October 23 to November 21
Sagittarius	November 22 to December 21
Capricorn	December 22 to January 20
Aquarius	January 21 to February 18
Pisces	February 19 to March 20

ARIES

The symbol for Aries might indicate the imminent arrival in the life of the questioner of a person born under the sign of Aries, but it could also relate to a time of fresh starts, the start of an enterprise, or even blind faith in the future. It might represent a leap in the dark or a pioneering attitude and a lust for adventure. Aries is connected to tools of all kinds, so a job that requires the use of tools might apply. Where health is concerned, Aries relates to the head and eyes, fevers, and headaches.

TAURUS

If the astrological symbol for Taurus does not refer to a person, it suggests putting down roots. The inquirer might buy or enlarge a home, or he or she might buy land and start to farm it. The questioner will certainly take an interest in money and might start to accumulate some of it, especially if there are dots close to the sign. Beauty in all its forms would appeal to the questioner, which might result in sprucing up his or her appearance, decorating his or home, or making a flower garden. The inquirer might become interested in music or cooking, carpentry or dressmaking. As far as health is concerned, Taurus rules the throat and cervical spine (neck).

GEMINI

Apart from indicating an encounter with people born under the sign of Gemini, this symbol could also represent education and enlightenment through books, training courses, college, or an IT starter course. Gemini relates to communication, so it might suggest a job in some field of communication. It can refer to neighbors, the neighborhood, and getting around locally, so if other aspects of the reading are referring to these things, this sign emphasizes them. Sometimes this sign refers to sports or games, especially intellectual pursuits, such as chess. As far as health is concerned, Gemini rules the nervous system, mental condition, hands, arms, shoulders, and upper respiratory system.

CANCER

This symbol might indicate the arrival of a person born under the sign of Cancer, but it could also hint at some change within the family. It could refer to or an event that affects the family or that brings the family together. This sign rules mothers and mother figures, so they might become important in some way. Cancer refers to the home environment, so a change of address is possible. This sign is also associated with small traders and small businesses, so these might shortly become central to the inquirer. An older school of astrological thought links this sign to travel, especially long-distance travel, so an important journey might be indicated. Regarding health, Cancer rules the thorax, lungs, and breasts.

LEO

Other than meeting a significant person born under the sign of Leo, the appearance of this symbol could also indicate some form of achievement that will bring acclaim. The questioner might pass an exam, finish a project, be asked to give a speech, take the lead in a play, or find some other way of shining and becoming a success. This sign also relates to children, especially the fun and pleasure that human beings get from being around them. It can relate to holidays and fun, sports and games, and even sexy love affairs that are not especially heartrending or serious. The health aspects of this sign concern the heart and spine.

VIRGO

This symbol might refer to a person born under the sign of Virgo, but it could also symbolize having to make selections and choices, to be discriminating about what is important and what is not. Virgo rules work and duty, employers and employees, so something to do with being employed or employing others might be important to the questioner. This sign also rules health and healing, so it might concern an ailment or it might indicate a growing interest in health and healing. In some cases, the inquirer takes up work or a pastime in some form of healing.

LIBRA

If this does not represent a person born under the sign of Libra, it could mean the start of a relationship, a marriage, or a business partnership. Love and sex might become important now but not in a hidden or damaging way. The questioner might take up a career in the beauty trade or find work in a restaurant or garden center. Sometimes the appearance of this symbol warns of an enemy, but at least this will be an obvious foe and not a hidden one. As far as health is concerned, Libra rules the pancreas, bladder, and nerves in the lower spine.

SCORPIO

The appearance of this symbol might indicate the arrival of a person born under the sign of Scorpio, but it might suggest making a firm commitment to something or someone through a marriage-type partnership or a working relationship. This sign rules such things as shared mortgages, legacies, taxes, and inheritance. It deals with birth, death, and the big events of life, such as marriage and divorce. It can also signal resentment, oppression, and tyranny, so the questioner must be sure that any new relationship that he or she enters into will not be detrimental. Health factors associated with this sign concern the reproductive organs, pelvis, lower spine, and eyes.

SAGITTARIUS

Other than indicating a new Sagittarian in the life of the questioner, the appearance of this symbol forecasts certain situations arising. This sign is associated with widening horizons, whether these are educational, spiritual, or literal. The inquirer might decide to look more deeply into spiritual, religious, philosophical, or ethical considerations, or he or she may start to travel, study, or expand his or her horizons in some other way. Ties and responsibilities may loosen while the questioner searches for the truth. Health issues relate to the hips and thighs.

CAPRICORN

Apart from new Capricorns entering the life of the questioner, the appearance of this symbol might indicate that business and finance are coming to the fore. The inquirer will work hard to achieve a particular goal. This sign could foretell a period of acclaim or of being in the spotlight and receiving awards for achievement. The inquirer may find him- or herself taking care of his or her parents or grandparents or taking care of other older people. The inquirer's own old age and the ailments that go with it may be a source of worry. Where health is concerned, the sign of Capricorn rules the knees, shins, and skin.

AQUARIUS

The appearance of this symbol can indicate that a new Aquarian might arrive on the scene, but it may signify a change in the inquirer's lifestyle. This symbol shows that this is not the time to be conventional and ordinary or to expect life to go along in the same old way. Some kind of breakout is on the way, in which original ideas and a new way of looking at life will be required. The questioner might start to take an interest in education, either as a trainer and teacher or by studying him- or herself. Aquarius rules the ankles.

PISCES

Other than a new Piscean coming into the questioner's life, the appearance of this astrological symbol might mean an inward journey and a search for meaning in life and the afterlife. There may also be an increased interest in art, music, and creativity or a desire to escape from the boredom of mundane work and duties. This symbol can also mean that you are in two minds about something, or that you just can't see things clearly yet. At worst, this is a warning not to escape into drugs and alcohol. The ailments associated with this sign relate to the feet and the liver.

6

TAROT CARD SYMBOLS

There are seventy-eight cards in a tarot deck, and nowadays there are literally hundreds of different decks to choose from, many of them with artwork that has traveled a long way from the original tarot designs. Therefore, if you think you see a tarot image in a cup, use your own knowledge of the tarot or look in a book on the tarot to see what it means. Meanwhile, here are meanings for a few of the more obvious images that you might come across.

MAGICIAN

This relates to a new enterprise and a bold step forward. The inquirer has the necessary skills and knowledge at his or her fingertips so is ready and able to put ideas into action. The Magician represents opportunities and the start of an enterprise or even a spiritual journey. Thought must be paid to new decisions and actions. There will soon be a chance to use skills and education in a practical manner, but there will be an element of politics, trickery, or salesmanship involved.

EMPRESS

The Empress combines sexual charms with being a loving partner and mother. If the questioner is female, this image may symbolize pregnancy and motherhood, but for either sex, this image can refer to a happy and satisfying marriage. There will be material satisfaction and comfort, along with full payment for work or efforts that the questioner makes.

If a change of address is indicated, there will be a comfortable home with land around it. Financial worries are at an end.

THE LOVERS

THE LOVERS.

Where the Lovers card appears, love, romance, and passion are coming, or a love affair that is worrying the questioner will soon blossom. On a milder note, this card also indicates friendship and harmony. If true lovers have been parted, this card is a good indication that they will soon be together again. Another interpretation indicates that the questioner will have to make a difficult choice.

JUSTICE

JUSTICE.

The Justice card suggests that the outcome of any situation will be fair and just. If there are legal matters to consider, the outcome may not be what the questioner would like, but it will be fair and reasonable. In partnership or business matters, responsibilities will be fairly shared and agreements can be reached. If the questioner has been wrongly accused, the situation will be put right and an apology will follow. The advice inherent in this card is to be aboveboard and completely honest in all dealings.

THE HERMIT

If an image of the Hermit appears, the inquirer may retreat from the social whirl. This image foretells a period of study, reflection, and the time and space to do some serious thinking. There may be a period of loneliness, convalescence from illness, or a period of working alone at home. Or the questioner might simply take time out from a busy life and enter a period of spiritual development.

WHEEL of FORTUNE.

THE WHEEL OF FORTUNE

The Wheel symbol could indicate journeys but it can also refer to changes of circumstances. If the inquirer has been in limbo for a while, change is on the way.

THE TOWER

The Tower image tells of something that will happen out of the blue, and it is not likely to be pleasant. Illusions will be shattered, and the truth about people and situations will be revealed in startling clarity. The inquirer will question previously accepted beliefs, and trust may be destroyed.

THE TOWER.

THE STAR

The Star is a symbol of hope, faith, and optimism, and it is a clear indication that things will go well in the future. If the questioner has been going through a particularly rough patch, life will soon become smooth again. Health will improve, and practically everything else will soon be better.

THE MOON

The central theme of the Moon symbol is illusion, delusion, mists, and mysteries. If the questioner has fallen in love, there may be illusion, obsession, and deception in the air. Where money and work are concerned, confusion, deception, and trickery may be prevalent, or it may simply be impossible for anyone to figure out what is really going on. There may be an untrustworthy woman around.

THE SUN

The Sun symbol indicates that joy and happiness are on the way. Whether marriage, health, work, money, or anything else has been worrying the questioner, it will all work out nicely now. A child may enter the inquirer's circle.

THE WORLD

The World symbol indicates a feeling of completion, of things coming full circle and the gradual and entirely natural end of a phase. Success and achievement are on the way, and the inquirer will have every reason to feel proud. There will be good fortune, spiritual enlightenment, and peace of mind. There may be travel for fun or business, or even emigration. A change of address is possible, as is any other change for the better.

ACES

All the tarot aces refer to the start of something new, and they are a generally lucky symbol.

Ace of Wands or Rods

This concerns business and work matters and creativity, so new ventures of all kinds are indicated here.

Ace of Cups or Chalices

ACE of CUPS.

This symbol can mean true love, a gift, or a good friend. It is all about people and feelings, and it is entirely positive.

Ace of Swords

This is a power symbol, so it suggests that the questioner will soon be able to make decisions and act upon them.

Ace of Coins or Pentacles

This symbol relates to money, security, growth, and business, so anything that is started now should increase in value and improve. A new source of income is possible.

Emperors, Kings, and Queens

These are adults in positions of power at work or within the family.

Princes and Knights

These represent lively young men.

Princesses

These represent lovely young women.

Pages

Pages represent children, messengers, or news. You will have to examine the rest of the reading to make sense of this image.

7

LETTERS AND NUMERALS

Letters of the alphabet that you see in a tea leaf reading refer to the name of a person, place, enterprise, or something else that is moving into the inquirer's life. This kind of symbol needs to be read in relation to others that are nearby. For instance, the letter *E* and an image of a house nearby could refer to a house name, such as "Elm," or the street that the house is on, such as Elm Road. A letter *J* close to a gun or dagger would warn that someone whose name starts with a *J* is gunning for the inquirer. The same idea can be applied to numbers, so if a number shows up, it is worth looking at what other symbols lie close by.

However, numbers have meanings of their own, and when we use the normal rules of numerology, letters can also have their own meanings. Here is the way that letters can be translated into numbers, so if a letter doesn't seem to link with anything or anyone specific, the number associated with it might offer some information.

A	B	C	D	E	F	G	H	I
J	K	L	M	N	O	P	Q	R
S	T	U	V	W	X	Y	Z	
1	2	3	4	5	6	7	8	9

NUMBER ONE (1)

This number represents a fresh start, so if the inquirer needs to tackle something difficult, he or she will have the energy and optimism with which to do it. This is a good time to sign a contract, finalize an agreement, or get started on project. The questioner should take time to talk things over with others, and then check out new ideas to see whether they will hold water. He or she should avoid haste and impetuosity.

NUMBER TWO (2)

The questioner should continue on his or her present path and consolidate what has been done so far. This is an excellent time to combine and cooperate with others or to seek help from them. Partnership issues should go well, but there can be conflict. The questioner should make time to relax.

NUMBER THREE (3)

This is an excellent omen for creative thinking and for coming up with problem-solving ideas, while artistic matters will also go well. The inquirer must avoid behaving in an irritable manner with others, but if he or she needs to stand up to others, this should be done in a direct and assertive manner without obstinacy or manipulation. There will soon be a time of socializing, parties, and outings. If the questioner needs to travel on business, for a shopping trip, or for fun, this will be a success.

NUMBER FOUR (4)

The questioner should focus on working and doing chores in a practical and constructive manner. Details will be important. The inquirer should also reach out to all those with whom he or she needs to cooperate, and the questioner should pay close attention to personal relationships and partnerships. There is a warning against riding roughshod over others while hurrying to get everything done on time.

NUMBER FIVE (5)

There is a feeling that one phase has ended and a new one is about to start. This shouldn't be a major change; it's just that one project is ending and another is beginning. There will be setbacks and interruptions but also a feeling of getting in touch with the right people. The inquirer will encounter new and interesting people, and a phone call or a letter could take the questioner by surprise.

NUMBER SIX (6)

Despite the fact that this number is often associated with hard work, there is evidence that the questioner will soon have time to enjoy nice meals, shopping for attractive things, and listening to pleasant music. Love and affairs of the heart will be well starred, and life will be good, but there is still work that has to be done.

NUMBER SEVEN (7)

Matters concerning love, passion, affairs of the heart, and relationships will come to the fore now. The questioner should focus on his or her love relationships, even if it means neglecting the chores, because there is something about the inquirer's personal life that needs attention. The inquirer should also go on an inward journey and contemplate spiritual matters. Studies and research will go well.

NUMBER EIGHT (8)

This number brings financial and business matters to the fore, so if the questioner needs to sort out loans or credit cards, pay bills, and get on top of money matters, he or she must address this now. Business matters will flourish, and there will be good advice and help from those in positions of authority. The questioner should spend some time alone, as he or she needs to concentrate on paperwork and details. One source of ancient wisdom says that the number eight suggests that the questioner might soon hear of a death.

NUMBER NINE (9)

The questioner needs to finish jobs that are hanging around and bring current cycles to a close, as there will soon be a fresh start. This is a good time to take a holiday or to look back on what has been achieved. The inquirer must be honest and fair in all dealings at this time.

TIME

A number might suggest a specific day or time, or it might refer to a place, such as the number of a building. Sometimes it is worth making a mental note of any number or letter of the alphabet that you see by noting it down on paper; then continue with the rest of the interpretation and come back to the number or letter later and see how it fits in with the rest of the reading.

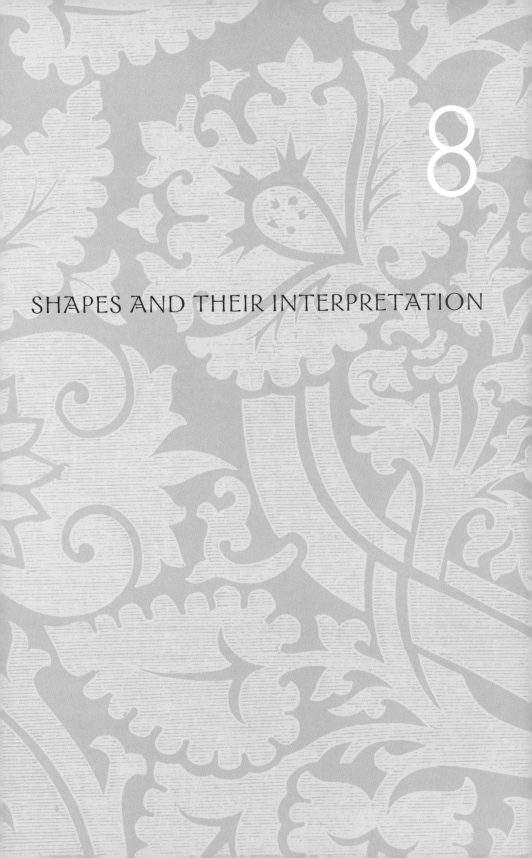

8

SHAPES AND THEIR INTERPRETATION

ABBEY: Throw caution to the wind because you can act freely without undue worry about the results of your actions.

ACE OF CLUBS: Keep a lookout for the postal carrier because a letter is on its way to you.

ACE OF DIAMONDS: You can expect someone to send you a gift, although it might not be diamonds!

ACE OF HEARTS: The ace of hearts indicates a period of happiness.

ACE OF SPADES: The ace of spades signifies a large building and a time when power is in your hands.

ACORN: The acorn is a very strong and auspicious symbol indicating happiness and contentment. From small beginnings can come enormous power! You can look forward to good health, success in business, and overcoming troubles. At the top of the cup, this sign means financial success and gain; in the middle, it brings improvement in health; at the bottom, it signifies good health.

ACROBAT: You can expect a turbulent period.

AIRPLANE: This sign is a good indication that you are about to soar to new heights, and there is a strong possibility of travel. Great fortune will come your way but not unless you take a gamble that doesn't seem to work out at first. If the plane is ascending, things are looking up. If it is descending, trouble is on the way. If the plane is broken, there is danger of accident. This symbol can also mean career advancement, and if it is close to the handle, it can denote an improvement in the home. When the symbol is on the side of the cup, the questioner wants to travel a long way from home. At the bottom of the cup, this symbol means disappointment in plans.

ALLIGATOR: You might need to hide behind a stern facade to escape danger. Beware of false friendship that is lurking somewhere in your professional life.

ALMOND: This shape signifies purity and virginity. There may be an alliance with a person born under the sign of Virgo.

AMBULANCE: This symbol denotes illness, and if it is near the handle, the sickness might be within the family.

ANCHOR: You need a well-deserved and comforting rest by water. Money matters look favorable. At the top of the cup, this sign indicates stability and dependability in love or business. If the anchor appears at the bottom of the cup, or if it is broken, it means instability and inconstancy. It can also

Anchor

symbolize an unpleasant situation or an encumbrance that is holding you back. At the side of the cup, this shape indicates a commercial venture involving travel. If there are dots nearby, this symbol is a very lucky one.

ANGEL: The angel is a sign of pure love and brings good news and spiritual protection.

ANKH: This symbol indicates a time of spiritual healing and wisdom.

ANKLE: This image signifies a time of instability and some form of immobility.

ANT: This sign represents hard work or indicates that a busy phase will end productively after a difficult period.

ANTEATER: After a rough-and-ready start, you will have some success, but it might be achieved in a controversial manner.

ANVIL: Hard and steady work is required for success.

APE: This symbol shows that you need to assert your strength in a more powerful way and stop copying the behavior or style of others.

APPLE: "An apple a day keeps the doctor away"; so goes the old saying. The apple is a good sign of health and vitality, together with creative or artistic achievement and abundance. You will reap the fruits of your labors. At the bottom

of the cup, this symbol advises you to guard against entice-
ment or overindulgence.

ARC: You need to take better care of your health if your plans
are not to be endangered.

ARCH: A positive opening or opportunity is arising. If the
arch is whole, your efforts are heading in the right direction,
and benefits can be expected or you can make a fresh start.
If the arch is damaged, you must review situations and make
necessary changes. In this case, you can look for added
meaning in symbols that appear near this one. This sign can
denote a good relationship or marriage to come.

Arch

ARK: You feel the need for safety and security, so this is a
time for you to withdraw from difficult situations and bring
your emotions back into balance.

ARM: Are you being too open or defensive about something? Open arms show that you need to be more open to
life. Closed arms suggest that you are being unnecessarily
suspicious about something. If the arm points up, you will
have new directions to follow. An arm pointing down suggests that it is time to motivate yourself. Horizontal arms
mean that you will help others or receive help from others.
If the arm is holding a weapon, you must take care, as enemies are around you.

ARMY: You will be involved in a controversial experience and
you will need to call on your inner resources to overcome
any obstacles.

**ARROW:** The arrow is a sign of clear direction, but it suggests that caution may be required. This symbol is also a sign of news, but it is worth noting the direction in which the arrow is pointing. If it points up, you will have luck in love. When the arrow is pointing down, you are taking the wrong direction in life. An arrow pointing in a horizontal direction means that you won't change but that you must be on guard against those whose attitude toward you is turning nasty. An arrow that is accompanied by dots shows that the trouble will be of a financial nature.

ASS: Misfortune can be overcome by patience. You may receive a legacy.

AX: The ax is a clear sign that you should take control of a situation. Is there something that you need to ax from your life? If the ax is near the cup's rim, you will overcome any difficulties. At the bottom of the cup, the ax tells you to expect danger and loss if you are careless. You might have to deal with a woman who could be described as a "battle-ax."

BABY: This symbol is a strong indicator that you are approaching a new, bright beginning. This development might be due to new interests that contain the potential for growth, or it might indicate the start of spiritual awareness. It can also indicate a yearning to be loved. At the top of the cup, this sign means that you will be the creator of a new idea. When this symbol is close to the handle, it signifies that a baby is on the way within your circle. At the bottom of the cup, this sign indicates that plans will not go ahead and that there will be minor worries.

BADGER: Is someone badgering you, or are you doing the badgering?

BAG: You are feeling trapped, or someone is actually holding you back or keeping you under his or her thumb. This sign can also indicate that you need to let go of thoughts or feelings that are no longer necessary. If the bag is open, you will escape.

BAGPIPE: You might pay a visit to Scotland, but in more general terms this symbol can be a warning of disappointment.

BALL: It's time to "have a ball"—go out, enjoy yourself, and have some fun. You feel restless and have a strong desire to

travel. It is time to take action. This symbol can also indicate a time of variable fortunes or deals that can bring unexpected wealth.

BALL AND CHAIN: You feel tied to commitments and obligations. If this symbol is at the bottom of the cup, it relates to hard times and a period during which you will have to work very hard for little return. A knotted chain indicates entanglements, while a broken one suggests that you will soon break free from a troublesome situation.

BALLOON: This symbol tells of a busy social life to come. If it is at the top of the cup, it will not be long before these busy times begin. If it is close to the handle, it means that you will marry, have a family, and settle down. If it is in the middle of the cup, you can expect success in middle age, but if the balloon is at the bottom of the cup, success will come later in life.

BANANA: This symbol denotes happiness and good luck.

BANNER: A banner signifies marriage to a successful partner, bringing respect, fame, and accomplishment.

BARREL: There will be a change in your financial circumstances. A whole barrel denotes good fortune and plenty of laughter ahead. If the barrel is broken or empty, there will be financial hardship and setbacks.

BASIN: You might have to work hard to keep yourself afloat financially. Additionally, there is a warning of illness or problems for a woman who is close to you.

BASKET: Cheer up! You will receive a useful gift or make a new friend. At the top of the cup, this sign represents a time of harvest, abundance, and material gain. Near the handle, it suggests that a new baby is on the way. If the basket is accompanied by dots, money will soon come your way. Flowers in the basket symbolize pleasurable times ahead.

BAT (animal): You fear the unknown, and this makes you sad, but this is a passing phase and you must learn to trust your intuition. You will soon be busy and productive.

BAT or CLUB: Beware of a situation that calls for watchful prudence.

BATH: It is time to cleanse yourself of your old way of life and change your behavior.

BAYONET: This symbol warns of a minor accident or some-one making a spiteful remark to you.

Bayonet

BEACON or LIGHTHOUSE: Expect to encounter a circum-stance calling for leadership or inspiration.

BEANS: This symbol represents money worries.

BEAR: A grumpy and difficult person is around you, and you will need strength, courage, and endurance to cope with this individual. A bear that looks more like a teddy bear sug-gests that something is going on in connection with children or childhood. You need close, loving contact in your life at this time.

BEASTS: This symbol is an omen of misfortune.

BED: You might miss an opportunity because of laziness. If you meet someone you want to become involved with for love or business, think carefully before establishing a close relationship or "getting into bed" in a business sense with the person.

BEE: The bee signifies fruitful hard work. If the sign is near the handle, there will be happiness and celebrations within the home. If it is approaching the handle, visitors can be expected. Away from the handle, it means that meetings will take place with a successful outcome. At the bottom of the cup, it means that there will be unfair criticism and allegations against you.

BEEHIVE: You can look forward to accomplishment in your work area.

BEETLE: The beetle is a good-luck symbol. You will experience renewal and growth, but there is a need for foresight. You will be given the opportunity for distant travel.

BELL: Your work or the services that you do for others will be recognized and rewarded. If the bell is at the top of the cup, there will be unexpectedly good news in love or business, but you must pay attention to detail. Two bells suggest that you can expect a successful romance or marriage.

BELLOWS: Renewed life will be pumped into something that has gone quiet.

BICYCLE: This is a time to show your individuality and to choose your own pathway.

BIRD: The bird represents good news or a message that is winging its way to you, particularly if the wings are open. If the bird is caged, there will be a feeling of restriction, but if the cage door is open, freedom is coming. Here are a whole host of bird interpretations:

Bird

Flock of birds:	Discussions will take place surrounding important or exhilarating news.
Flying bird:	Good news is coming soon, and you may travel.
Standing bird:	Delays can be expected.
Chicken or hen:	You will enjoy a happy home life. This can also foretell hearing of a death.
Crow or raven:	The crow or raven is a bad omen and a warning; take time to relax.
Dove:	The dove represents a time of peace and love.
Eagle:	Power and transcendence are yours.
Goose:	The symbol of a goose predicts prosperity and happy times with family and friends
Owl:	A time of insecurity; a journey is possible.
Parrot:	Beware of idle gossip.

Peacock:	The peacock represents pride and display from either you or others.
Rooster:	The rooster warns of a boastful person, but it also suggests that you wake up and seize the moment.
Swallow:	The swallow is a sign of love and new beginnings.
Swan:	This symbol has a variety of traditions and meanings, which are listed in this tealeaf dictionary under the word "swan."
Vulture:	Beware of loss, theft, jealousy, treachery and trouble.

BIRDCAGE: Frustrating difficulties will hold you back.

BIRD'S NEST: A bird's nest signifies a happy family life. Eggs in a nest indicate a nest egg to come or the birth of children. A broken nest tells you to expect family discord.

BLUEBELL: You need to open your eyes and discover what is going on around you.

BOAT: You will be moving on in your life soon, but you need to be cautious while doing so. If the image is at the top of the cup, a worthwhile journey will be undertaken, your ship is coming in, and you can expect a visit from a friend. A capsized boat denotes danger through upsetting circumstances or because you are let down by an undependable friend.

BOMB: A volatile situation is looming. Beware of your own emotions because they are about to explode.

BONES: A situation around you calls for inner strength and spiritual resilience.

BOOK: Check your datebook. Is there something that you have forgotten to book—a particular appointment, maybe? If the book is open, there will be good news and an answer to a question. If it is closed, there is a question to be investigated. If there is a tea stalk near the book, tradition says that there will be marriage to a writer. A book and pen indicate that you will make a living by writing.

BOOMERANG: Beware of repercussions. This is a warning not to gossip because it will rebound on you.

BOOT: Changes are entering your life. If the boot is near the handle, there will be changes in the home area. If the boot is away from handle, the changes will occur within your social life. If the boot is at the top of the cup, there will be protection from pain or loss; if it is in the middle, there will be travel in connection with your work; but if it is at the bottom, you can expect to become unemployed.

BOTTLE: Temptation might surround you, so consider this before taking the plunge into something stupid. Are you bottling something up? There is a volatile atmosphere around you that requires caution, so do not overindulge yourself in anything. At the top of the cup, this image can

signify festivities, but when it is at the bottom, you must watch your health.

BOUQUET: You can look forward with pleasure to a happy event, which could be a romantic interest or validation for your work or talents.

BOW: A bow is a lucky symbol meaning reward or celebration of accomplishment.

BOW AND ARROW: A bow and arrow warn of jealousy, rumors, slander, and bad news around you.

BOWL: This sign brings invitations, money, or abundance.

BOX: Are you feeling boxed in? Now is the time to face your fears and get away from what you feel is restricting you. If the box is open, you will soon receive a gift. If it is closed, something you thought lost will be found.

BRANCH: It is time to branch out and create new growth.

BREAD (LOAF): Bread represents nourishment, but it shows that this is the right time to think seriously about your health and to evaluate your diet.

BRICKS: Bricks are a sign of power and fortitude. This sign represents a time in which to create good foundations for steady growth.

BRIDGE: The bridge is a powerful symbol for transitional

changes that can represent a new job, relationship, career, or home. Satisfaction can be achieved. A problem will soon be solved through a life-changing event or person. (Look for nearby symbols for additional information.)

BROOM: You are entering a new era in your life where old difficulties will be swept away. This is the chance to begin anew. "A new broom sweeps things clean." There is a need for improvements or decoration to your home or work environment. Clear the clutter now.

BUBBLES: You need to lighten up and learn to enjoy life. Bubbles floating on the surface of your drink tell of money that is coming in.

BUCKET: The bucket represents a time of hard work in either a marriage or a committed relationship.

BUCKLE: A buckle signifies defense and protection. Partnerships will be successful.

BUD: This sign indicates immaturity or unformed plans.

BUFFALO: This symbol represents great supremacy and abundance.

BUGLE: You need to prepare yourself for a difficult venture ahead.

BUGS: Insects always indicate a host of problems, but none of them are large or overwhelming.

BUILDING: It is time to create new foundations in your life, or there could be a change of address.

BULL: You have hidden reserves of strength, so take control of a situation. Arguments and bad feelings may be encountered (the direction the bull is facing will show whether this is coming toward you or moving away from you). There might be an important contact with a person born under the sign of Taurus, or you might need to develop Taurean qualities within your own life.

BULLDOG: There is a need for tenacity. You need to stand firm and defend yourself.

BUSH: You will encounter an obstruction to new opportunities. Branches signify choices.

BUTTERCUP: You should live in the country rather than the city.

Butterfly

BUTTERFLY: The butterfly is a powerful sign that suggests a new beginning (think of the butterfly emerging from its cocoon) and a time of rebirth. It is the bringer of love and happiness wherever you go, and it signifies some long overdue joy. However, beware of fluttering from one relationship to another. If there are dots nearby, beware of frittering your money away. If this sign is at the bottom of the cup, you will have a short-lived love affair.

CABBAGE: Envy and spite are working against you. If there are dots nearby, the problem is at or around your place of work.

CACTUS: A thorny situation will require courage and stoicism.

CAGE: Are you feeling trapped? There is no need to feel like this, as you have various options open to you. It is time to change your way of thinking and to remove the restrictions you have imposed upon yourself.

CAKE: It is time to indulge yourself and to celebrate. You have a wish that will be fulfilled and festivities to enjoy.

CAMEL: You will overcome burdens and anxieties in order to reach sanctuary.

CANDLE: You will soon see the way forward, and you can expect help from friends.

CANDELABRA: You will find a solution to problems.

CANNON: Help is coming through powerful friends. There may be news arriving from someone in the armed forces. If there is a star near this sign in the cup, promotion is likely.

CAP: Trouble is coming, so beware of speculation and be careful in whom you trust.

CAR (automobile): The future is somewhat unstable, so look before you leap. If the design of the car is clear, there will be travel. If the sign is broken up, expect some mechanical trouble.

CARPETS: You can enjoy being with true friends and take pleasure in happy social activities.

CARRIAGE: There is approaching wealth and visits from friends.

CART: You will experience fluctuations of fortune.

CASTLE: This sign offers security and protection. A wish is granted, but if the castle is in ruins, hopes and dreams will not come to fruition.

CAT: Follow your heart, but guard against ruining your chances by being hard to please. Beware of deceit from an untrustworthy friend. A sitting cat means good luck.

CATAPULT: There will be arguments and discord and an unprovoked attack.

CATHEDRAL: You can look forward to great prosperity.

CATTLE: Prosperity is coming your way.

CAULDRON: There are sacrifices to be made.

CHAIN: If the chain is clear and well formed, a fortunate undertaking or serious commitment will be a great success. This sign can also relate to news of a marriage or engagement and happiness to come. If the chain is broken, you can expect trouble in relationship matters.

CHAIR: Take the time to relax and enjoy yourself. Expect a guest or new addition to the family. With dots around it, this symbol tells of a financial improvement.

Chain

CHARIOT: You will experience success in business matters provided you use control.

CHERRY: The cherry is a good omen for love, especially for a younger inquirer.

CHESSMEN: Concentration is needed.

CHEST: Is there an area in your life that you need to open up to? This symbol represents undiscovered potential.

CHESTNUT TREE: You will either receive justice or give a fair hearing to someone else.

CHICKEN: Make sure that you have set yourself realistic goals, and think about the situation more deeply. Easter could be a significant period.

CHILD: You need to deal with previously unresolved childhood issues. This sign can also mean the birth of a new idea or the start of a family.

CHIMNEY: Beware of hidden danger.

CHRISTMAS TREE: This sign represents good luck around Christmastime.

CHURCH: Faith in divine providence brings blessings with unexpected benefits.

CIGAR: It is time to release your anxieties, as you will meet a new friend or have a new business relationship. If the cigar is broken, there will be losses.

CIRCLE: This powerful symbol shows that it is time to look at a situation in a completely new way. If the circle is whole, there will be success, a possible wedding, and completion. A broken circle (like the shape of the letter C) means that a temporary offer will come, or there will be tentative offers without fruition. Two circles indicate two marriages, while circles with dots nearby relate to a baby. If there are three dots, the child will be a boy.

CLAW: The claw is a clear warning that there is danger around you from hidden enemies.

CLERGYMAN: This sign heralds the end of an argument. There may be a church event such as a wedding or a christening, but if this sign is at the bottom of the cup, there will be a funeral.

CLIFF: Be prepared for a big change that might mean taking a risk without knowing the outcome. Beware of pitfalls, as this can be a critical time.

CLOCK: This symbol is telling you that it is time to take care of your own health or that of someone else. It is also a warning against procrastination, because this is the right time to move on with things. If the clock is at the bottom of the cup, this means that you will hear about a death.

CLOUDS: Do you have your head in the clouds? Problems need careful handling. Small and fluffy clouds are a happy omen, but thick and dark ones represent gloom and sadness. Dots around the clouds mean that there will be numerous problems.

CLOVER: You finally receive the good news that you have worked hard for. A clover with four leaves means very good luck.

CLOWN: Enjoy yourself, laugh, and be in high spirits. You can look forward to uncomplicated pleasures and joy.

COACH AND HORSES: You can look forward to an increase in status.

COAT: This sign denotes the end of a partnership or friendship.

COCKEREL: Others see you as dependable rather than intelligent, but you will gain respect in later years. If the cockerel is at the bottom of the cup, guard against arrogance.

COFFEEPOT or TEAPOT: A special visitor is coming, but this is not the start of a romance.

COFFIN: Great care must be taken. There may be news of a loss.

COIN: A lump sum of money is coming your way. The coin is an excellent sign of good fortune in all money matters. (See also the section on the Ace of Coins in Chapter 6, "Tarot Card Symbols," in this book.)

COLUMN: Expect to receive promotion and success, provided your ego does not get in the way. Helpful friends will assist you. A broken column is a warning about an untrustworthy friend.

COMB: You need to improve your appearance. You have enemies around, and while you may know who they are, you must keep an eye on what they are doing if you can.

Comet

COMET: You are on the brink of a critical change or dramatic event in your life. Beware of loss or theft.

COMMA: Rest and relaxation are necessary.

COMPASS: What direction do you need to go in? Do you feel lost or confused? Do not despair, because you will soon have a change of direction and an opportunity to travel.

CORK: You can look forward to a time of parties and celebrations.

CORKSCREW: You will be unable to take the direct route. This is a warning that there are untrustworthy people who are around you.

CORN: Rewards are approaching, and you will reap what you have sown.

COUCH: Great wealth can be yours if you are wise and shrewd.

COW: This is a time for peace, abundance, and prosperity, along with some form of fertility—perhaps in the form of a good idea or two.

CRAB: Are you being too emotional or bad tempered? It is time to be more direct and to keep an eye open for devious people. This symbol can also mean that someone born under the zodiac sign Cancer is coming into your life.

CRADLE: A stranger is coming. This could literally mean a birth or a renewal of old friendships.

Crescent

CRESCENT: The crescent is a lucky sign because there will be success in financial affairs and a journey over water. A crescent moon with a star nearby is exceptionally lucky, while a new moon signals a good time to make changes.

CROCODILE: Be wary of hidden danger, either from your own self-undoing or via someone else.

CROCUS: Stay alert, as good fortune is around you.

CROOK (shepherd's staff): The crook is a sign of protection, but you need to exert leadership qualities.

CROSS: There is a choice to be made that will bring a dramatic change. Suffering or a sacrifice is indicated here. If the symbol is near the cup's rim, the change will come soon, but if it's at the bottom, the change will come later. If the cross is shaped like the letter *T*, you can look forward to hard-won success and happiness. A cross in the shape of an *X* is a warning of danger. A broken cross symbolizes obstacles and losses.

CROWN: A crown is a very lucky sign. You can look forward to accomplishment, respect, and luck that come without your having to make any special effort. You will receive respect and recognition for your talents. A crown with stars represents unexpected luck.

CUP: There are many meanings associated with this sign. One meaning says that leisure and pleasure will put you to unnecessary expense. Another advises patience rather than asserting yourself. There could be a reward in the form of written praise or a gift. Finally, a new friend is in the offing.

CUPID: Love is on the way.

CURTAIN: Secrets hide behind the curtain.

CUSHIONS or PILLOWS: This sign is a caution against laziness and procrastination.

CYMBAL: The cymbal warns against artificial love and broken promises.

DAGGER: There are dangers around for yourself and others. Beware of a jealous person who wants to make trouble. Guard against speaking sharp words or revealing personal information, and be aware that there may be hidden dangers or offers that are too good to be true. Do not be too hasty.

DAFFODIL: A daffodil is good sign, indicating new beginnings. Excellent friends are around you.

DAISY: If there is a choice to be made, you should choose simplicity. There will soon be a new love or a happier time within an existing relationship.

DANCER: Your wish will be granted.

DANDELION: Unless you are cautious, you will experience inconvenience in your travel arrangements.

DASHES: You might take several short trips that are a waste of time.

DEER: You should be more assertive and try to overcome shyness. The deer is a good omen for studying or taking exams.

DESK: A letter will bring good news.

DEVIL: This sign denotes commitment to a project or a hot, passionate love affair.

DIAMOND: A gift or windfall is coming your way.

DICE: Dice signify a time of destiny and change. You need to go with the flow. If negative signs surround the dice, avoid gambling.

DISH: If the dish contains food, it symbolizes domestic comfort, unless the symbol is at the bottom of the cup, in which case it means that there will be trouble at home.

DIVER: All will soon be revealed to you.

DOG: You may want to be a lover, but you can only be a friend. If the dog is at the bottom of the cup, a friend needs your help. A barking dog warns of an untrustworthy friend. This symbol can also mean that someone who was born in the Chinese zodiac year of the dog is coming into your life.

DOLPHIN: Help will be given in an emergency. It is a safe time to travel, and you will be welcome wherever you go.

DONKEY: This symbol indicates stubbornness and endurance. You need to demonstrate more patience and understanding. A donkey near the cup's rim represents good luck and a possible legacy. If the donkey is at the bottom of the cup, you must be prepared to make sacrifices.

DOOR: You are entering a new chapter in your life. Expect something strange to happen. Be aware of opportunities that will be around you.

DOORBELL: You may expect good news.

DOTS: Dots usually refer to money and often need to be linked to nearby symbols.

DOVE: Peace is coming. The dove is also a good omen for domestic life.

Dragon

DRAGON: The dragon signifies new beginnings, but you need to face unforeseen problems head-on. You may come across a scheming or flashy person. This symbol may relate to someone born in Chinese zodiac year of the dragon who will become important to you.

DRAGONFLY: There will be positive events within the home.

DRUM: This is a time for a change. If the drum is near the cup's rim, you can work toward a powerful position in life, but if it is at the bottom of the cup, you can expect quarrels and conflict.

DUCK: You may have been frivolous when young, but you will calm down with age and when you find the right partner. You will have a devoted companion, and you will receive news of money coming your way.

DWARF: Is there something overwhelming you? Do not put limits upon your potential. Be tolerant when defusing situations.

EAGLE: You may be obliged to do boring work or to spend time doing things for others, but if you look at this situation from a different perspective, you will see that there is a point to it. A change of address could be on the cards.

EAR: Pay attention, because you will benefit from something you hear. You may hear a secret or two.

EARRING: A luxurious phase will soon begin.

EASEL: This is an ideal opportunity to learn artistic skills. Dots around the easel mean that money will come your way.

EGG: If the egg is whole, there will be new life or a successful new beginning. If it is cracked or broken, you will experience failed plans or financial problems, but these can be overcome.

EGGCUP: Danger has now passed, so you can start to relax.

ELEPHANT: This symbol signifies wisdom, strength, and good mental health. Love and passion will come your way, as will affection and tenderness. If something is taking time to sort itself out, you will need patience.

ENGINE: Some news is coming your way very soon.

ENVELOPE: Good news. You will receive a long-awaited letter or important paperwork. A letter of the alphabet or a number on the envelope will indicate from whom or when it will come.

EXCLAMATION MARK: It is time to pay attention to what is going on around you, but you must also guard against impetuous actions.

EYE: This symbol means that you will soon be able to see how to solve a long-standing problem. Be cautious, keep your eyes open, and look carefully at what is being offered to you. Others may envy you.

FACE: It is time to face up to a situation. Is someone around you being two-faced? (Look for nearby initials for clues to the identity of the person.) A face near the cup's rim or its handle is a warning against too much introspection. If this sign is facing another symbol, it emphasizes the importance of that symbol. A smiling face symbolizes friendships that bring happiness and joy. An angry face means that you will soon have to deal with angry, difficult people.

FALCON: Embrace the success that is to come.

FAN: This sign indicates indiscretion and playful flirtation, but you mustn't take this too far.

FEATHER: If the feather is near the cup's rim, amazing good fortune is on its way to you. If it is at the bottom, you will suffer artistic blocks and a lack of concentration.

FEET: You will soon need to make an important decision and perhaps take a new direction in life.

FENCE: Are you feeling fenced in by temporary and self-imposed restrictions? You may experience minor setbacks but nothing lasting or permanent. It is time to be decisive.

FERN: You will experience a period of irritation, restlessness, and frustration.

FERRET: This sign warns of active enemies around you.

FIG TREE: The fig tree is a lucky sign signifying good events to come.

FINGER: This sign suggests that either you or someone else is pointing the finger of blame. If the finger points up, caution is required, and if the finger points down, it is time to stop whatever you are doing with your life and change direction.

FIR TREE: You can look forward to success in creative matters.

FIRE: This sign is a clear indication that you will experience passion, hot emotion, and sexual desire. At the top of the cup, this sign also represents achievement, while at the bottom of the cup it signifies that you are in danger of being too hasty.

FIREPLACE: You can expect happiness in the home.

FISH: The fish is a symbol of good fortune. It shows that you need personal freedom in order to develop hidden talents. This sign can relate to sharing knowledge or to a teacher. Travel and movement also come with this sign. There could also be a connection with a person born under the sign of Pisces (especially if there are two fish).

FLAG: Wave good-bye to your problems, as long as you are prepared to be more assertive. You also need to be alert to danger (look to nearby symbols for added meaning).

FLATFISH: You should hide from view during times of danger.

FLOWER: A flower is usually a happy omen, and if it is near the cup's rim, praise and compliments will be coming your way. In the middle of the cup, it means that love and marriage are on the way, but if it is at the base of the cup, it means that for the time being, you will be unhappy in love.

FLY or FLIES: A fly or flies represent minor setbacks. There is also an annoying person within a domestic situation.

FOOT: It is time for movement in love, career, or location.

FOREST: This is a perplexing time. You have too many pressures and you feel overwhelmed; you can't see the forest for the trees.

FORGET-ME-NOT: You can't forget someone, or you yearn for someone to remember you.

FORK: Do you have to make a decision about something major? Beware of false flattery—get advice from trusted friends before making your decision. If the fork points up, you will experience new interests, but if it points down, an old problem will reappear.

FORKED LINE or FORK IN THE ROAD: You have reached a crossroads, and there are two pathways forward from which to choose.

FORT: You will soon be in a strong position.

FOUNTAIN: This sign is a strong indicator of a permanent relationship with everlasting love and overflowing happiness.

FOX: Are you being outfoxed? A cunning person may be trying to trick you. You have the wisdom to lead and advise others.

FOXGLOVE: You give time, affection, and gifts to others with a joyful heart.

FROG: This sign brings fertility and abundance, even in the form of a disguised handsome or beautiful lover, but beware of being inconsistent.

FRUIT: It is time to reap the rewards! Prosperity, fertility, and success will come to you.

GALLOWS: Not unexpectedly, this symbol warns of danger and bad luck.

GARDEN: You will go to a party or celebrate something.

GARGOYLE: Beware of a deceitful person who will cause problems.

Garland

GARLAND: If this symbol is at the top of the cup, it symbolizes happiness in relationships; if it's at the base, it foretells a funeral.

GATE: Be aware of new opportunities around you. If the gate is close to the cup's rim, there will be an opportunity to obtain information and knowledge, to enjoy new experiences, and to achieve future success. At the bottom of the cup, this sign predicts problems. Take care.

GEESE: Surprise visitors and invitations will arrive.

GIANT: This symbol indicates a strong person who may be in a position of influence or authority.

GIRAFFE: Lack of thought or discretion may cause difficulties.

GLADIOLI: Gladioli signify triumph and achievement. They can also indicate a possible Australian connection.

GLASS: You can look forward to celebrations, parties, and social events, unless the image is at the bottom of the cup, which means that others may question your integrity.

GLOBE: Do you want to travel the world? This sign indicates long-distance travel.

GLOVE: It's time to "take the gloves off," as a challenge is presented to you.

GOAT: You will climb upward and eventually reach your goal, but you must watch out for enemies. Your persistence will pay off, but you must take some time to rest and relax. Is there a person born under the sign of Capricorn who needs your attention?

GOLF CLUB: This is a time for business mixed with pleasure.

GONDOLA: A lover or deep friendship is promised, as is travel.

GOOSE: You can expect prosperity, a time of plenty and good times with friends and family in the future.

GRAPES: Celebrate! It is a time of health and happiness, as well as invitations to happy events and a few good meals out.

GRASSHOPPER: Stay with one thing at a time and finish what you start. You are in danger of living for today and not taking care of tomorrow. Enjoy a reunion with an old friend.

GREYHOUND: Good luck and fortune can be obtained, but only by strenuous means.

GUITAR: You may become involved in a musical group. You will be happy in love.

GUN: Do you feel the need to protect yourself from danger, discord, and quarrels? There are stubborn enemies around, a bully, anger, and hidden dangers or violence. You need to be extremely careful for a while.

HAM: "Ham it up" with happy family social events.

HAMMER: Hard work is needed to accomplish anything you truly want, which may mean abandoning old, unfinished tasks for new ones. More assertiveness will reap benefits.

HAMMOCK: This image shows that it is time to relax.

HAND: Hand symbols usually refer to love, but they can concern life in general. Here are a few variations on the theme of the hand:

Hand

- An open hand signifies protection and/or help from a friend. It also means that you are in the hands of fate or destiny.
- If the hand is closed, beware of an argument or closing yourself off from new prospects. (Look for added meaning among symbols that the hand points to.)
- A thumb pointing up denotes a time to go ahead with plans; a thumb pointing down means that you should wait.
- Two clasped hands signify friendship.
- If the hand is at the bottom of the cup, you will need to control your emotions.

HANDCUFFS: This sign warns of restrictions and difficulties.

HAND MIRROR: You will experience enlightenment through dreams.

HARE: The long-eared hare represents something important brewing in your future relating to love or travel. However, beware of becoming overconfident. If the hare is at the bottom of the cup, a shy friend needs help.

HARP: There will be romantic harmony and success in love.

HAT: While spotting a man's hat in a tea leaf reading is said to be an unfortunate omen, a woman's hat is said to bring luck, honor, and fame. Your efforts will be recognized and rewarded, especially in a new job. You will experience a change in roles or business success.

HAWK: There is jealousy around you, but you must ensure that you are not the envious one.

HEAD: There is a new opportunity ahead, but you need to take time to scrutinize the situation.

HEART: The heart is the sign for true love, happiness, or financial gain. If the heart is at the bottom of the cup, take care of your health.

HEATHER: This symbol signifies good luck.

HELMET: There will be a fight or passionate love affair—or both.

HEN: You can look forward to a very happy home life.

HILLS: Beware of making mountains out of molehills. There are minor challenges to be faced, but they will leave you feeling better once you have dealt with them.

HIPPOPOTAMUS: You can look forward to passion once your shyness has been conquered.

HOE: Hard work will be rewarded.

HOLLY: This sign represents good luck, particularly around Christmastime.

HONEYSUCKLE: You will experience love and fondness that will last.

HORN OF PLENTY: Abundance is coming your way, but be cautious about spending it all at once.

HORSE: Impatience may spoil your chances. If the horse is galloping, there will be good news. If there is also a rider, the news will come from overseas. If just the head of the horse shows, you will soon have a lover in your life.

HORSESHOE: The horseshoe is a sign of good luck. You will have success if you proceed with your plans, particularly travel arrangements.

Hourglass

HOURGLASS: You need to decide to do something within a specific period. Keep an eye on those who are dear to you. This is also a warning for you to be punctual.

HOUSE: You cannot rely too much on others because you need to look after your own interests. You cope with stress well and can even overcome trauma. If the house symbol is near the cup's handle, there will be some domestic problems. If it is at the top of the cup, there will be a change of address, but a holiday or a short time spent away from home is likely if the house is in the middle area of the cup. If it is at the bottom, take care with everything.

HUMAN FIGURES: Pleasure and happy times are coming. (Look to other symbols nearby.)

ICEBERG: You are in danger of drifting without emotional direction. This could lead to a slowing down of projects or plans coming to a sudden halt.

INKPOT: Understandably, this sign represents a letter.

INSECT: What is bugging you? This is an indication of distractions and broken concentration. You need to be calm in order to focus. You will easily overcome a number of minor distractions providing you remain tranquil.

IRIS: Your wealth will be found far from home.

IRON: Problems can be worked out if you press on!

ISLAND: Are you isolating yourself? This is a time for you to reassess where you want to be, but this sign can also indicate an enjoyable holiday to come.

IVY: This is not a good time to be too independent; allow your friends to help you.

JACKAL: You must become more aware of your surroundings and of those who are around you, because there may be someone who wishes to make mischief.

JESTER: Enjoy yourself by all means, but beware of making yourself look like a fool.

JEWELS: This symbol is a strong indication of material success. It also means that you will receive a precious gift.

JOCKEY: Take a chance, because you are going to be lucky and enjoy a winning streak.

JUDGE: It is time to evaluate a situation.

JUG: At the top of the cup, this sign indicates good health, but if it is at the bottom of the cup, it warns against extravagance. When the jug is elsewhere in the cup, it means that you are about to reap the rewards of someone else's efforts.

JUGGLER: Do not be taken in by others, but rely on your own skills. You will soon have your hands full and be juggling your time and responsibilities, possibly due to promotion or a new job.

KANGAROO: It is time for you to leap ahead, but do not reveal your innermost feelings to those who are critical or false. You will enjoy harmony at home. Travel is also strongly indicated.

KETTLE: If this symbol is near the handle, it represents domestic comfort, happiness, and a special visitor. The visitor might be a friend or a relative, but he or she is unlikely to be a lover. If the kettle is at the bottom of the cup, it denotes a minor illness.

KEY: There will be good news. You may hear news about a change of address or a new love affair. Crossed keys represent recognition and success in romance, while a bunch of keys tells of happiness in all areas. At the bottom of the cup, keys warn of a possible robbery.

KEYHOLE: You can expect something new to start very soon, and you will be lucky in love. If the keyhole is at the bottom of the cup, you will want to make changes and find love, but you will meet only with frustration for the time being.

KING: This sign is a strong indicator of people in authority, so you might improve your position at work with help from a powerful friend. Alternatively, you may become a powerful person in your own right.

KITE: Set your sights high and focus on your wishes, because they will be granted.

KNAPSACK: You will take a useful journey, although if the knapsack is at the bottom of the cup, this will not happen for a while yet.

Knife

KNIFE: There are a number of meanings associated with this sign, depending upon the condition and position of the knife.

- Good or bad aspects of your life will be magnified.
- Take care not to use sharp words or reveal personal information to the wrong people.
- Cut away the deadwood, and clear the clutter at home or in your workplace.
- Beware of someone who is deceitful.
- If the knife points away from the cup's handle, it signifies a broken friendship.
- A knife at the bottom of the cup warns that legal matters will go awry.
- If there are two crossed knives, you will feel helpless.

KNIGHT: Someone strong is coming your way, and if appropriate, this will be a new lover.

LACE: You will soon make progress.

LADDER: Your life will improve, and you may be given a promotion or see an improvement in a business situation. Missing rungs indicate setbacks but not a complete loss. A ladder at the bottom of the cup warns of financial loss.

LADLE: Working partnerships will be harmonious.

LADYBUG: The ladybug is a very lucky sign, so you can expect a windfall.

LAMB: Are you being too meek? It is time for you to become more assertive. If the lamb is close to or facing the cup's handle, it predicts a time of plenty, especially of the things you want and need within the home and domestic environment.

LAMP: If the lamp is at the top of the cup, it predicts a feast and a time for you to shine. If the symbol is at the side of the cup, secrets will be revealed. A lamp at the bottom of the cup symbolizes postponement, while two lamps suggest that you will be married twice.

Leaf

LEAF: There are several meanings attached to this symbol.

- This is the time to turn over a new leaf.
- You can expect a letter or message bringing good news.
- A new life or lifestyle is on the way to you, and a trans-forming event will end the old one, so it is time to let go of something.
- Happiness in the home is indicated, along with an unex-pected financial gain.

LEG: It is time to take a stand and then move forward in life.

LEMON: This symbol warns of jealousy or bitterness.

LEOPARD: You will need to be strong and somewhat cunning if you are to achieve success. You will take a long journey soon.

LETTER: Check your mail! You will receive a long-awaited let-ter or important paperwork. The position of this sign will show whether this delivery contains good or bad news. With dots nearby, this sign means that there will be money to come. With a heart nearby, the letter sign means that there will be emotional or marital problems.

LIGHTHOUSE: Hidden dangers will be exposed.

LIGHTNING: Astonishing events or insights will come.

LILY: You need to work toward a dream, and if the lily is near the top of the cup, the dream will come true. Health and happiness will also come your way, but there will be anger and strife if the lily is at the bottom of the cup.

LINES: Lines always represent journeys, but the length and condition of the line will tell you whether the journey is long or short, straightforward or full of problems.

LION: This is a time for you to take control of things and to reassert yourself. Bold, swift action will take you a long way, but at a price. Influential friends will be around. A male lion represents a powerful contact or important man, or it may represent a person born under the zodiac sign of Leo. A lioness represents a strong family.

LIZARD: Pay attention! Do not believe all you are told, but trust your own instincts.

LOCK: There are blockages in your way.

LOG: If lit, this symbol means warmth and companionship. If unlit, it represents wasted opportunities.

LOOM: The pattern of events will soon become clear.

LOOP: Avoid impulsive actions, and look at things carefully before voicing your opinions. If the loop is well formed, there will be a happy undertaking or serious commitment. If it is broken, you can expect trouble or disruption.

LUGGAGE: The traditional meaning associated with this sign is of a journey that will bring good luck or perhaps of emigration. This symbol also suggests that you need to let go of old habits.

MAGNET: You will attract good things to yourself.

MAN: Not unexpectedly, this image has several meanings:

Man

- Perhaps you need to tap into some form of masculine energy.
- Traditionally, this shape represents a visitor of either gender, and if the image is clear and distinct, the person will be dark, while a vague figure represents a fair person.
- This shape near the handle represents a close friend or relative coming to visit.
- If the symbol has an outstretched arm, it is bearing gifts.
- If the figure is opposite the handle, someone will soon be working very hard outside the home.
- If the figure is facing away from the handle, the person might be leaving.

MANSION: You can expect an increase in status.

MAP: Anything resembling a land mass or recognizable continent refers to the influence this place will have in your life. This sign could indicate a connection with that area, a journey, or a need to map out your future.

MAPLE LEAF: This is not the time to squander opportunities. There may be a connection with Canada or a suggestion that the autumn will be a good time to make headway with your plans.

MASK: Are you hiding behind a mask? Are you happy with yourself, or do you need to change things? This symbol shows that a highly strung and insecure person craves your attention. Take care with secrets.

MAYPOLE: Springtime brings changes for the better.

MEDAL: You can look forward to a reward.

MELON: Happiness and prosperity abound.

MERMAID: Is there someone you like who is unattainable? Resist temptation and beware of hidden enemies.

METEOR: A successful venture or increase in status is on the way, as long as you don't allow the opportunity to slip away.

MONK: This symbol means that you should get some rest and spend time on inner reflection.

MONKEY: The monkey is a sign that it is time to play and be free! Be yourself. You are gifted and capable, and your gifts can bring joy to others and fame to you. Try not to gossip or spread rumors. You might become involved with someone born in the Chinese zodiac year of the monkey.

MONKEY PUZZLE TREE: It is time to cut out the deadwood in your life and to clear the clutter from your home.

MONSTER: Seeing this sign is similar to dreaming about monsters; it shows that something is worrying you and that you should take a serious look at it before it becomes too big to handle.

MOON: This is a good sign for romantic attachment or deep friendship. If the moon is surrounded by dots, there will be a marriage based on material matters rather than love.

MOTH: Is there something eating away at you? You might be obsessing over someone or something, and if you don't get a grip on yourself, you will make yourself and others unhappy.

MOUNTAIN: This symbol represents great achievement after a period of hard work and living through some hard times.

Mouse

MOUSE: This symbol suggests several things, all of which relate to being in control of our own environment and life:

- You should not allow others to make your decisions for you.
- You must avoid deceitful or larcenous people.
- It is easy for you to attract lovers and friends, but you must ensure that they are right for you.

MOUTH: Are you communicating with others in the right way? There may be a gossip in your environment, or you may be in danger of saying the wrong thing yourself. You will hear something to your benefit if you stop talking and start to listen.

MUG: You can look forward to celebrations with visitors.

MULE: Be patient and don't be too stubborn. Maybe you need to lighten your burden.

MUSHROOM: Expect a rapid rise in status and some success. At the top of the cup, this image denotes a journey or a move to the country. At the bottom of the cup, it means rapid growth. If the mushroom is upside down, there will be frustration through business difficulties or problems within the home.

NAIL: Take some time to reassess your plans and projects. Someone may act unfairly toward you or make you angry, or you may experience some kind of emotional pain in the near future.

NECKLACE: This image relates to your love life, and it means that you will be happy in love and marriage-type partnerships, but a broken necklace means a love relationship will come apart. Much the same can apply to friends and friendship; that is, you will have good friends as long as the necklace is whole.

NEEDLE: You will receive recognition and admiration, but you may need to repair a relationship that is going wrong.

Net

NET: You need to be aware of a trap. Are you taking too many risks?

NUN: There is a need for self-control and restriction, and you need some time to yourself so that you can think things over. You will receive some friendly female advice.

NURSE: Care is needed in the areas of health and well-being.

NUTCRACKERS: Any difficulties you may be experiencing will disappear.

120

OAK TREE: You can look forward to a long life, steady progress, and good health.

OAR: You may feel emotionally out of balance, but there is success in store after a period of trials.

OCTOPUS: Beware of becoming entangled in a messy situation. There is danger around you, and someone may be keeping important matters from you.

ONION: This sign warns you to keep some things to yourself. It also predicts that you will become successful in later life.

ORCHIDS: A passionate affair is on the way, but if the orchid is at the bottom of the cup, it indicates obsessiveness and destructiveness.

ORGAN: Do you want harmony or discord? The option is yours.

OSTRICH: Don't bury your head in the sand. If this symbol is at the top of the cup, you will soon take an important journey. If it is at the bottom of the cup, you will still travel, but later rather than sooner.

OWL: You appear to be wise, but you are often lost. Beware of gossiping about others or becoming the victim of gossip. At the top of the cup the owl brings good news, but if it is at the bottom, it indicates scandal and deceit.

OYSTER: You are on the point of starting a new relationship that will be filled with passion. You will make money, but later rather than sooner.

PADLOCK: If the lock is open, you can expect a surprise, but if it is closed, it symbolizes a warning.

PAIL: Clear up loose ends before commencing anything new.

PALACE: Marriage for money brings an increase in your status.

PALM TREE: This symbol indicates happiness and contentment for the whole family, and even a touch of luxury. You may take a nice vacation.

PANSY: You will cheer up a despondent friend.

PANTHER: This shape warns of betrayal and deceit from a trusted friend.

PARACHUTE: You will have a lucky escape.

PARCEL: You will receive a gift and an increase in wealth.

PARROT: This is an indication of insecurity, but it can also mean that other people are talking about you. A journey is also indicated.

PEACOCK: Are you being too proud or boastful—"as proud as a peacock"? Although you may not have much luck right now, you tend to bring luck to others—and that will bring you karmic benefits later.

PEAR: This sign indicates a comfortable life with ample money.

PEN: This is a time for communication. You will soon have to write some letters.

PENDULUM: This is a sign of uncertainty and changes in direction. You will spend time with laid-back friends, and you will soon be able to relax and ease your anxieties and tension.

PENGUIN: You will hear from someone from the south or will be traveling southward yourself.

PENKNIFE: You will loosen some ties. Others will not be in a cooperative mood.

PEPPER POT: This sign shows that a manipulative person will create arguments.

PESTLE AND MORTAR: Medication will be required to treat an illness.

PHEASANT: There is a promotion or an inheritance coming, but there may also be a legal loss.

PHOENIX: "The phoenix rises from the ashes." This is a time of recovery and rebirth. A lover will return, and a past project can be revived successfully.

PICKAX: Be careful, as there are strikes and dissension at work.

PIG: You will soon improve the lives of others, and the good you do will live on. Beware of a greedy or jealous person, and guard against overindulgence. There may be a connection to someone born in the Chinese zodiac year of the pig.

PIGEON: You will hear news from overseas.

PILLAR: Do you feel the need for support, or do you have to support others? You will either provide great friendship or receive friendship from others.

PINEAPPLE: Your dreams will come true.

PINE TREES: You will be happy.

PIPE: Joy and freedom are within your grasp, bringing luck in love and a happy life. A kind man may solve a problem, so do not be suspicious of his motives.

PISTOL: This is a warning of danger.

PLAIT: Your life will become entwined with another's.

PLOUGH: You will need patience while working on a project, but it will be worthwhile in the end.

PLUM: A new and excellent opportunity will come your way, and you will have to take a journey in connection with it.

POLICE OFFICER: You are being protected and will receive assistance from those in authority. Release any guilt that you may be feeling, as it is not productive.

POPPY: Do not put off things until tomorrow. If this shape is at the bottom of the cup, it is a symbol of pain and loss.

POSTAL WORKER: Important news is coming, and the sign's position will tell you when, because the nearer the cup's rim the symbol is sitting, the sooner the good news will come.

POSY: Love and romance are indicated. If a ring or bell is nearby, there will be a wedding.

POT: This symbol represents service to others. If you have made a start on a project, it will be some time before it takes off.

PURSE: If the purse is closed, you will gain something soon. If it is open, and especially if it is near the bottom of the cup, you will lose something. If there are dots around the purse, you will soon be involved in a profitable venture.

PYRAMID: You can expect achievement after hard work. This sign also denotes spiritual enlightenment.

Pyramid

QUEEN: You will meet an influential woman who will be helpful to you. If the symbol is at the bottom of the cup, she will be meddlesome and malicious.

QUESTION MARK: This image symbolizes a need for caution, so you may need to reconsider your plans or question your own motives.

QUILL PEN: Documents will need to be signed.

Rabbit

RABBIT: This symbol contains several meanings:

- This sign symbolizes prosperity, but you may need to be brave and assertive in order to prosper.
- You need to slow down and become more organized.
- You should use your excellent communication skills to good advantage.
- There will be fruitfulness in family or business matters.
- There could be a connection with someone born in the Chinese zodiac year of the rabbit.
- This sign could mean that Easter will be a significant time.

RACKET: You will receive an invitation to a social gathering.

RAILWAY: This sign means you will take a long journey.

RAINBOW: A rainbow is a wonderful sign indicating that you are on the right path and that your wish will come true. It signifies the end of any difficulties. Similar to an arch, it represents the path between your world today and your destiny.

RAKE: You should avoid raking over old grievances. If something has been hidden from you, you will soon discover what it is. A relationship might end when secrets are revealed.

RAM: Now is the time to implement new ideas or projects. Someone born under the sign of Aries might become significant to you.

RAT: Beware of treachery, dishonesty, and loss. Be particularly wary of friends or lovers. Someone born in the Chinese zodiac year of the rat might become important to you.

RATTLE: Children will bring delight.

RAVEN: The raven is a strong warning symbol of bad news and especially of hearing of a death.

RAZOR: This is a time to be extremely cautious about accidents, arguments, threats, or separations.

RECTANGLE or SQUARE: You will face a challenge or difficulty, but you will also have spiritual protection. Look to nearby symbols, especially symbols within the shape, for added meaning. This symbol can represent protection from harm, but it can also refer to restriction and to being stuck in one place for a while.

REPTILE: There will be deceit from trusted friends.

RHINOCEROS: Charge ahead but keep your secrets to yourself.

RIDER: Expect to receive good news of great significance and to be lucky.

RIFLE: All firearms are a symbol of danger, discord, and strife.

RING: Not unexpectedly, this sign relates to marriage and marriage-type relationships.

Ring

- At the top of the cup, this symbol represents a marriage or a proposal of marriage.
- If the ring is at the bottom of the cup, there will be a relationship but no marriage.
- If the ring is broken, the relationship or marriage won't last.
- If the ring is complete, the relationship will be fine.
- If a broken ring looks like a letter *C*, an offer won't reach fruition.

Road

ROAD: In tea leaf readings, roads and paths are always a metaphor for your journey through life, and this symbol can refer to your current lifestyle or the near future.

- Two parallel lines mean that your situation is about to change.
- Straight lines show that the way forward will be easy, while wavy lines denote difficulties that can be overcome.
- A fork signifies two choices.
- A bend represents unexpected events.

ROBIN: In just about every tradition, seeing a robin means that you will receive news of a death, but in some cases, it can signify that a situation could be ending. However, it also means that you will have luck during the winter.

ROCKET: You have unlimited power to achieve, and this will bring you and your loved ones much happiness.

ROCKS: You need to become more grounded. There is hidden danger, but you will scramble over obstacles.

ROLLING PIN: This sign denotes an industrious period, but it also brings disagreements within the home.

ROOF: This symbol signifies a change of address or a new relationship.

ROSE: This old symbol has gathered a lot of meanings in its time:

Rose

- There is popularity, love, and great affection to come.
- There will be a new romance or a deepening of love.
- Someone will ask you to bring together those who have shared a secret in the past.
- If the rose is at the bottom of the cup, there will be setbacks in love and delays.

RUG: This sign represents happy social events and true friendship.

RUNNER: Are you running away from something? Perhaps you need to face up to something. You can also expect to receive messages and news. At the top of the cup, the runner brings good news, but if he is at the bottom, he will bring sad news.

SADDLE: Are you feeling "saddled" by a situation? It is time to release the burden and mentally ask your spiritual guides or your higher consciousness to bring you changes for the better, travel, and new prospects.

SAILOR: There will be news from across the water.

SAUCEPAN: This symbol is a warning that anxieties can be expected.

SAUSAGES: Sausages foretell a time for wining and dining and generally enjoying yourself. If the sausages are near the handle or toward the top of the cup, you can expect some enjoyment in the home.

SAW: What needs to be sawed away? Perhaps you need to cut yourself away from external interference or cut yourself off from disruptive influences. It seems that something needs to be removed in order for you to move forward.

SCALES: Scales symbolize legal matters or something that feels like a court case, in that you are advised to prepare your case carefully. If the scales are balanced, justice will prevail, but if they are unbalanced, you could expect an unjust result. This sign also indicates a possible involvement with a person born under the zodiac sign of Libra.

SCALLOP: It's hard to believe, but this symbol means that the fairies will guide you if you let them! Relax, imagine light and energy coming down from the universe and going through you, and see if you receive some kind of message or insight from your fairy guide.

SCEPTER: This symbol shows that power and authority are on your side.

SCISSORS: It may be time to remove yourself from a situation or a relationship because of quarrels and unrest. Cut trouble out of your life.

SCORPION: A person born under the zodiac sign of Scorpio will have an important influence upon you. Take care because Scorpios always have a sting in their tails.

SCYTHE: The scythe is a warning symbol, as it shows that you are in danger from a possible accident.

SEAGULL: You will go far so long as you are not weighed down by too many responsibilities.

SEESAW: There will be ups and downs in finances, but you can expect a successful outcome.

SERPENTS: Beware of spiteful enemies, bad luck, or illness.

SHARK: A shark is a strong omen of danger. Beware of bankruptcy.

SHEEP: This ancient symbol has a number of meanings:

- It is time now to use your own judgment and not allow others to dictate to you.
- Look at the choices that you can make and focus on the right one.
- Good fortune and prosperous times can be had, but beware of those who might attempt to defraud you.
- You need to be calm and peaceful.
- You must try to control unhelpful emotions and impulses.
- It is possible that you will receive help from someone born in the Chinese zodiac year of the sheep.

SHELL: Are you feeling discontented and keen to hide away? Do not despair, for good news is on its way and you will soon be lucky and successful with both money and love.

SHELTER: This image is an indication of possible danger, loss, or ill health.

SHEPHERD: Guidance and help are on the way, and if the shepherd is accompanied by sheep, good fortune is coming as well.

SHIP: There will be news from a distance or a worthwhile journey over water, and your ship is coming in. At the bottom of the cup, this symbol means that you can expect disappointment.

SHOE: Put your best foot forward, because a change for the better is coming and you are on the correct path, but don't make changes just for the sake of it.

SIGNPOST: See where this image is pointing and interpret the symbols nearby, as these will be particularly important.

SKELETON: There will be financial losses or the loss of a friend. Take care of your health. Skeletons that have hidden in the closet might soon start to emerge.

SLUG: Your wishes will be granted.

SMOKING CHIMNEY: "Where there's smoke, there's fire," they say, so this symbol warns of danger around you or perhaps a lack of clarity. You need to clear your thoughts. If the smoke rises straight up, everything will go well. If it bends sideways, there will be limitations and boredom.

SNAIL: Are situations moving too slowly? Perhaps you need to get moving. You will leave your mark, but you must proceed carefully.

SNAKE: Just as a growing snake sheds it skin, this is a time of transformation for you. Beware of someone who does not deserve your trust or of hidden enemies. This sign can refer to the start of a passionate affair.

SPADE: Do the groundwork on a particular project and then work on in a steady manner and it will all turn out well.

SPARROW: This symbol says that love and affection are coming your way, along with good news about your finances. At the bottom of the cup, this sign can indicate hearing about a death under strange circumstances or discovering hidden enemies.

Spider

SPIDER: There are several meanings associated with this sign.

- Insects and small animals denote many small problems.
- You must look within yourself and view things from a different angle.
- You will soon be rewarded for hard work.
- Look out for a crafty character.

SPIDER'S WEB: "O, what a tangled web we weave, / When first we practice to deceive." This sign is a clear warning to keep away from traps or manipulation. It is also a potent symbol of fate.

SPOON: This lucky symbol can signify a flirtation or perhaps comfort from your family, but its traditional meaning is a birth. Two spoons might mean twins or perhaps a marriage proposal. Frankly, any event that comes your way over the next year or two will be a happy one.

SQUARE: This symbol is a sign of stability. You will receive protection from loss or harm, although restrictions and adversity may have to be endured.

SQUIRREL: You are being advised to take care of your finances or your supply of energy and to be frugal with both. You must prepare for some difficult times ahead.

STAG: For a female, this symbol means that a strong young lover is on his way. For a man, this symbol means that friendship will be more important than romance or even sex for a while.

STAIRS: Expect an increase in status or in spiritual awareness.

STAR: This ancient symbol contains several meanings:

Star

- The star is a sign of hope, love, joy, and prosperity.
- If the star has six points, it means that your dreams will come true.
- If the star is five pointed, there will be an increase in spiritual consciousness.
- Small stars at the top of the cup symbolize talented children.
- A large number of stars represent problems with finances but with a successful outcome.
- A single star at the bottom of the cup advises you to change direction before it is too late.

STEEPLE: This symbol signifies some slight delay and a small patch of bad luck.

STICKS: These symbols represent people. If the sticks are crossed, there will be arguments and partings. If there are leaves clustered around the stick, there will be bad news. Dots or small leaves around the stick show that someone will bring money your way, while a ring nearby is said to represent a future marriage.

STOCKS: Beware of an embarrassing situation.

STORK: A birth! This sign can indicate the birth of a child, particularly if it is near the handle. If it is far from the handle, the stork represents the birth of an idea or a new scheme. Either way, this is a good omen for family happiness and contentment.

STRAWBERRIES: There will be good times ahead, with an improvement in your finances. There may also be a marriage proposal.

SUITCASE: There are visitors approaching, and travel is strongly indicated.

SUN: This sign denotes a new beginning and enterprises that will flourish, bringing happiness, comfort, good health, and power. A child could be of importance. A person born under the sign of Leo could be significant. Summertime is likely to become a significant period.

SUNDIAL: A serene time is ahead.

SWALLOW or SWIFT: This symbol usually relates to travel, so you can expect changes to come because of travel, or you might take an interesting trip just for the fun of it. You may even embark on a lifetime of travel. Near the cup's handle, the swallow offers protection for the home and family.

SWAN: There are several meanings attached to this symbol, so you will have to see which one applies to your particular situation.

Swan

- You will experience a troubled time, but you will have the sense to escape before it develops into anything serious.
- There may be an unexpected and unusual lover.
- There will be an improvement in finances.
- If the swan appears at the bottom of the cup, you might hear of a death or you might separate from a long-term companion.

SWORD: The sword is a powerful sign denoting arguments and problems, divorce, illness, or death. You need to remain in control. If there are two crossed swords, you must avoid using sharp words or revealing personal information, as this will lead to arguments and battles. If the sword is broken, you will experience a defeat.

TABLE: If you need to make a decision, don't hesitate in doing so. This sign can also signify a happy social interlude, family contentment, and social or business gatherings. If the symbol is near the cup's handle, there will be celebrations within the home. If it is surrounded by dots, there will be discussions about money.

TAMBOURINE: This symbol registers a time of merriment and fun.

TEAPOT: Your happiness is to be found within the family and home.

TELEGRAM: You will receive sudden news, possibly coming from afar. (Look at the other symbols nearby to determine whether the news will be good or bad.)

TELEPHONE: Expect an important call. (Look at the other symbols nearby to determine whether the call will bring good news or bad.)

TELESCOPE: Adventure awaits! It is time to make plans for the future.

TENT: It is time to get away from everyday life and get back to nature. This sign can indicate physical travel or spiritual journeys of self-awareness.

THIMBLE: There will be changes within the family circle, and you should focus on nurturing your domestic life.

THISTLE: You will encounter a tough person who can endure anything, and you will soon need to find courage within yourself. There can be good news about love.

TIGER: It is time to draw upon your own energy. You will be able to see straight through people and therefore be able to influence them. Expect good luck in speculation.

TIMBER: Logs of timber are an indication of success in business.

TOAD: Watch your emotions and do not be easily flattered.

TONGS: A period of sleepless nights, restlessness, and frustration is inevitable.

TORNADO or WHIRLWIND: Prepare yourself for a turbulent period.

TORTOISE: You will overcome problems by slow, sure, and determined efforts and by being very patient. Someone will criticize your work but will do so in a constructive manner, so the criticism will be beneficial in the long run.

TOWER: Are you feeling isolated? If this sign is near the cup's rim, it means that you are building something that will last, but at the bottom of the cup, the tower can indicate a risk of failure or a sudden disappointment.

TRAIN: You have the power to reach your goals. There will be steady gain throughout your life, and you will meet many interesting people. If the train is at the base of the cup, it denotes an unfortunate journey.

TREE: This ancient omen has gathered several meanings along the way. Read them all and see which applies to your situation.

Tree

- Expect positive improvements in your way of living and to have your wishes fulfilled.
- You will recover from an illness.
- You will renew old friendships, but you must avoid being put in a position where you make needless sacrifices for others.
- If the tree is isolated, this sign relates to heritage, lineage, and possibly an inheritance.
- If there are no leaves on the tree, you can expect family conflict.
- Many leaves on the tree mean that you can enjoy family contentment.
- A group of trees signifies family unity, and if they are evergreen, relationships will last.
- A palm tree signifies wealth and perhaps a beach vacation.

TRIANGLE: The triangle is the sign of protection and of a lucky surprise. If the point is facing down, take care if you happen to be in a love triangle. If the triangle is wedge shaped, someone will get in the way of your relationships.

TRIDENT: Something connected with the sea will bring good fortune.

TRUCK: You will be moving around the world during your later life.

TRUMPET: Expect to hear an announcement.

TRUNK: You will take a journey that will have a dramatic effect.

TULIP: Tradition gives this flower an odd meaning. It advises you to seize an opportunity that comes your way and then move swiftly away from possible danger.

TUNNEL: You will soon start to see where you are going.

TURKEY: The main meaning for this sign is pretty obvious, as it symbolizes a time of family gatherings and festivities. However, if it is at the bottom of the cup, planned festivities will not work out.

TURTLE: You have a large job on hand and you mustn't rush it. There are times when your nerves will get the better of you, and then you will want to withdraw.

TUSK: You will be lucky in love.

UMBRELLA: The umbrella is generally a sign of protection. If the umbrella is open, you will get what you want, but if it is closed you will not. If it is inside out, there will be temporary problems. If the umbrella is at the bottom of the cup, it can show that you and your family need more protection than you have. Perhaps this is a time to review your insurance policies?

UNICORN: This symbol denotes a secret relationship or marriage, as well as spiritual guidance and luck.

URN or VASE: This sign is a good omen for luck and for spiritual development and friendships, so it is an all-round good symbol. The only slight warning is to avoid putting yourself to unnecessary trouble for others.

VIOLET: Violets are always a symbol of great love and a happy home life. According to legend, Napoléon Bonaparte had violets planted on St. Helena as a symbol of his love for the wife and family that he could no longer be with.

VIOLIN: There are people around you who are arrogant and bigheaded. These people might also be too independent. Whatever they are like, you need to move away from them because they will only make you unhappy.

VOLCANO: Unsurprisingly, this sign relates to upheavals and arguments. Watch your tongue and your temper.

VULTURE: Do you need to clear up a messy situation? Is there someone around you who acts like a vulture? Beware of loss, theft, jealousy, and malice.

WAGON: This symbol relates to childish pleasures, fun, simple amusements, and sometimes more complex ones, such as weddings or holidays. If the wagon is at the bottom of the cup, you may have to put your plans on hold for the time being.

WALKING STICK: There will soon be a male visitor.

WALL: You need to get out more.

WASP: Has someone stung you by his or her words or actions? Beware of egotism. You could experience romantic problems.

WATERFALL: You can expect happiness, wealth, and prosperity.

WAVY LINES: You may lose your way or experience losses and aggravation.

WEATHER VANE: Beware of indecisiveness.

WEDDING or WEDDING CAKE: You will have a wedding to attend.

WELL: Inspiration is yours, and a wish will be fulfilled.

WHALE: The size of this creature forms the symbolism. For instance, you might take on a large project, or you could forgive a great wrong or settle long-standing family problems, or you might set out on a long journey. These things might be real or symbolic—for instance, you may take a long inner journey rather than a real one.

WHEEL: Events outside your control will change the direction of your life. If the wheel is complete, there will be good fortune. If it is broken, there will be disappointment and delays.

WHEELBARROW: You will need to rely on yourself and avoid telling lies or half-truths.

Wheel

WHIP: As long as you are not too overbearing, you will have the upper hand.

WINDMILL: You need others to do some work for you or to do something on your behalf. This will happen and will work out well.

WINDOW: You will soon see where you should be going. If the window is open, you will soon start to explore new horizons, but if it is closed, you may opt for something nearer home. If the window is dirty, your luck will not be as good.

WINE BOTTLE or WINEGLASS: Enjoy celebrations, but don't overdo things.

WINGS: Wings are a good sign, denoting freedom. There will be messages, gifts, or some form of news. If you are working toward a specific target, you will hear good news in connection with this sign. Do not box yourself in or limit yourself unnecessarily.

WISHBONE: Your wish will be granted.

WITCH: Expect a strange occurrence.

WOLF: There are several meanings attached to this ancient symbol, so you need to determine which is the most appropriate.

Wolf

• You need to maintain balance within a family situation.
• You are in need of emotional support.
• Beware of jealousy, and be cautious about those you trust.
• Someone will challenge you or betray you.
• Guard against obsessive feelings or being overwhelmed by your own feelings of jealousy.

WOMAN: If the figure is clear and uncluttered, you can look forward to harmony and happiness. A clouded figure denotes bad omens and jealousy from a woman. Also look at the symbols nearby for clarification.

WORMS: This symbol warns of scandal. Beware of someone trying to "worm his or her way" into your circle.

WREATH: If this sign is at the top of the cup, it is a good omen, but if it is at the base, it brings news of a death.

YACHT: Expect an easier lifestyle and good financial position, but take care that you are not at the mercy of someone's whims.

YEW TREE: If the tree is at the top of the cup, you can expect to be rewarded later in life for the work that you do now. If it is at the bottom, it denotes a death or a separation. If there are dots nearby, you can expect to receive an inheritance.

ZEBRA: Be more flexible and adventurous in your travel plans. A love affair will be exciting and enjoyable so long as it remains hidden.

conclusion

By now you will have discovered that it is not difficult to read the leaves. Some of you have an artistic and visual eye, which makes it easy for you to figure out the shapes in the cup. You may wish to note down the shapes and then look them up in the tea leaf dictionary section in this book once you have given the cup a good going over. In time, you will build up your own personal dictionary, and your interpretation of certain shapes may be different from those in this book. This is normal, because good readers always develop their own ideas as to the specific meanings in time. This applies to tea leaves, tarot cards, numerology, and much else, because it is the personal touch that makes these readings so magical.

Some of you will find that even when you are not in the process of giving readings, your intuition about people and situations starts to expand and develop. You may even find yourself becoming clairvoyant or clairaudient. Clairvoyance is the ability to see things in the mind's eye and to obtain a mental impression, while clairaudience is the ability to hear spiritual messages.

There aren't really any downsides to tea leaf reading, but bear in mind that people take what they hear seriously. Even if they pretend to be blasé or to laugh it off, you can be sure that they are taking in what you say—and they will remember it afterward. It is important not to frighten your questioner. Tell him the truth about what you see and feel, but if you think the news is particularly bad, perhaps give up some of your "integrity" and soften the message. Professional readers know that the information that they receive from the tarot, from tea leaves, or from their spiritual guides can sometimes be "over the top" and too harsh. They know that the problem that they see can turn out to be less black than it appears in the reading. It is entirely possible to pick up on someone's worry or unsettled state of mind and think that this indicates some future disaster. So do take care.

The only other downside is that you will become too good at tea leaf reading. So what's the problem with that? The problem is that the world and his wife will soon be at your door, asking you to read for them, leaving you with little peace or time to yourself. At this point, you can choose to become a professional by asking your "clients" to pay you a little money for their readings or you can learn to say no. You will still want to give readings to those who truly need your help, but you will start to weed out those who just fancy being amused or entertained. In essence, there is nothing wrong with wanting to be amused and entertained, and nothing wrong with you doing this for your friends and acquaintances. However, all forms of reading can be tiring, so moderation is the key. You need to enjoy giving readings and you will want others to get something out of them, but you don't need to become a sucker. I hope you truly enjoy your reading and eventually pass on your knowledge to others.

index

Note: Please also refer to the dictionary
of shapes and interpretations (pages 67–150).